THE

CHRISTIAN
CLEANSING

OF AMERICA

Unless otherwise specified, all Scriptures are taken from the King James Version of the Holy Bible.

The Christian Cleansing of America
© 2013, Noah W. Hutchings and Carol Rushton

Printed in the United States of America

ISBN 1-933641-49-5

THE
CHRISTIAN
CLEANSING

O F   A M E R I C A

Noah W. Hutchings
with Carol Rushton

Contents

"Barack knows that we are going to have to make sacrifices; we are going to have to change our conversation; we're going to have to change our traditions, our history; we're going to have to move into a different place as a nation." —Michelle Obama

Introduction

The subject of this book may be somewhat confusing to some, as cleansing is usually understood to be an effort to remove by washing something that is unsightly or unclean. "Christian cleansing" in reference to our present time relates to current efforts or attempts to remove from life in the United States the identification with anything that relates to the Bible, church, or individual faith in Jesus Christ as the Son of God who died for the sins of the world. This Christian cleansing process is evident in the news media, in government, in entertainment, in sports, etc. This effort must be placed within the context of what God has said about the generation that would be in the world in the last days before the Second Coming of our Lord and Saviour, Jesus Christ.

> When the Son of man cometh, shall he find faith on the earth?
> —Luke 18:8

I could continue and give hundreds of scriptures relating to the apostasy in the churches, sinful world conditions, and the rejection of everything that related to the prophetic signs of the last days, but this would be another book. Those interested may be referred to one of my other books on this subject: *Forty Irrefutable*

Signs of the Last Generation; commentaries on Daniel and Revelation; and *Is the Antichrist in the World Today?*

Also, I will not try to document the Christian faith of our founding fathers like Benjamin Franklin, George Washington, Patrick Henry, and others. This, too, would make another book. Those interested in more information on this subject may obtain a copy of *America's Christian Heritage* by Pastor Paul Blair, or any of several books by David Barton. There are also many other documentaries on this subject. The fact that our founding fathers had unquestionable faith in God, the Bible, and the Lord Jesus Christ is beyond question. The influence of the early Pilgrim and Puritan settlers from England is the base of our national history. As settlers spread across the nation from east to west, the first building that was erected in a community or town was a church building. The Ivy League, now identified with sports, was originally established to train ministers for the purpose of evangelizing the new nation. The *World Almanac* acknowledges that the population of the United States is seventy-eight percent Christian and two percent Jewish.

I say the preceding to prove that President Obama's worldwide announcement that the United States is no longer a Christian nation is a lie, or at least wishful thinking.

According to the tenth chapter of Genesis, and other scriptures, God divided the nations and set the bounds of their habitation. Today, there are over two hundred member nations in the United Nations. During the past 2,013 years, nations have warred against each other over boundaries or for political, economic, or racial reasons.

After World War II, the United Nations was formed as a forum where representatives from all nations could meet and peacefully discuss and settle differences, thus eliminating war, hunger, poverty, etc. However, the U.N. became nothing more than a debating arena, or a forum for third world nations to accuse the United States for their problems. However, the U.N. has done little to settle or negotiate the differences between nations. Since the founding of the United Nations, the United States has been involved in the Korean War and the Vietnam War. There has been almost continual war between Israel and the Islamic world, as well as revolutions and regional wars in Asia, Africa, South America, and various other parts of the world. Also, the major nations have stockpiled fifteen thousand deliverable atomic or nuclear warheads capable of destroying life on earth.

These continuing problems of mankind have provided a reason and emphasis for a new form of world government in which the present systems of economics, politics, and religions would be completely changed. This new international arrangement on a national basis is referred to as the "new world order."

The forming of this new world order brings us to the fulfillment of the biblical prophetic warnings of the establishing of such a system in the last days where all nations and people would be under the rule of one man, one religion, and one economic system; everyone would worship this person, and there would be one business permit, called the "mark of the beast." All religious differences would be resolved by declaring them illegal. Everyone in the world, according to the prophetic Word, will worship this one man as a god or have their heads cut off according to Revelation 19–20. Once this world ruler is worshipped as the god of a new international religion, he could then resolve all political and economic problems by cutting off the heads of all dissidents. It is interesting that the most common method of execution in the Islamic world is beheading.

To illustrate the increasing rejection of basic Christian faith, morals, and worship in the United States, I collected the following news reports, which I think the reader will find most interesting. Rather than quote the articles referenced, I have summarized the contents of each article.

> **Poll: Religion's Influence Waning in America**
> (ChristianPost.com, December 30, 2010)—Gallup polled 2,048 Americans. The same Gallup poll in the 1950s indicated that almost all Americans thought their Christian or religious faith was very important in their personal lives. The latest Gallup poll indicates that seven out of ten Americans believe that religion, including Christianity, was not of great importance in their lives.

> **Christmas carols = bullying?**
> (OneNewsNow.com, December 26, 2012)—Complaining parents in Montana want Christmas carols in school replaced with secular songs.

> **Bloomberg Stands By Decision to Leave Out Clergy at 9/11 Ceremony**
> (FoxNews.com, August 26, 2011)—A Christian minister was not welcome at a ceremony honoring the dead of the terrible 9/11 tragedy.

> **Atheists Ask Obama to Ditch "So Help Me God," Bible in Presidential Oath**
> (ChristianPost.com, November 14, 2012)—Evidence of con-

tinuing efforts not only to try to enforce the ambiguous policy of "separation of church and state," but to separate the nation from God.

> **Critics Slam U.S. Government, Media for "Weak" Response to Anti-Christian Attacks**
> (FoxNews.com, February 15, 2011)—Criticism of president for failing to mention in communications with Islamic leaders the growing persecution of Christians in the Muslim world in which sixty-five Christians have been killed recently.

> **Free speech vs. sound of silence**
> (OneNewsNow.com, December 11, 2012)—ACLU threatens to sue Miami-Dade government for voting to allow a moment of silence for prayer before county meetings.

> **Watching Internet Porn at NYC Libraries Protected by First Amendment, Officials Say**
> (FoxNews.com, April 25, 2011)—Public libraries in New York City now make porn available to its patrons.

> **University Pays Up for Expelling Christian**
> (WorldNetDaily.com, December 10, 2012)—Eastern Michigan University had to pay for dismissing a counselor who refused to counsel a homosexual.

> **Jon Stewart and Gene Robinson strike out on Bible, family**
> (OneNewsNow.com, December 14, 2012)—Promotion of a book promoting homosexual marriage by Episcopalian bishop Gene Robinson.

> **Something missing from WWII memorial**
> (OneNewsNow.com, November 9, 2011)—The words in President Roosevelt's prayer for U.S. soldiers landing on Normandy beaches in WWII, "Almighty God" and "so help us God," have

been removed from a WWII memorial in Washington, D.C. Like deletions have been made in the prayers and speeches of former presidents—alarming examples of Christian cleansing!

> **Texas woman forced to cover up "Vote the Bible" T-shirt at polls**
>
> (FoxNews.com, November 1, 2012)—The voter did not endorse either candidate, but the incident emphasizes the declining respect for the Bible in the American general public.

> **Wal-Mart Worker Says She Was Fired for Praying With a Crying Customer**
>
> (ABCNews.com, December 14, 2012)—A Wal-Mart clerk was fired for trying to pray with a distressed customer.

> **Christian groups finding hostility at colleges**
>
> (Baptist Press [bpnews.net], November 28, 2011)—Four Christian groups were kicked off campus by Vanderbilt University in the enforcing of a new policy that no organization at the university can suggest or hold any members or leaders to moral standards, beliefs, or behavior.

> **DAR Denies They Are Censoring Prayers**
>
> (FoxNews.com, January 4, 2013)—Are the Daughters of the American Revolution removing Jesus' name from prayers and books? Although the organization denied the charge, the article contends that a thorough scrutiny of the *Missal & Ritual* book on organizational prayers and procedures indicates that in every place where Jesus Christ was referenced in the old edition has been removed in the new edition.

> **Town's Christmas cross replaced with "holiday tree"**
>
> (OneNewsNow.com, November 28, 2012)—Freedom from Religion Foundation was successful in having a Christmas

cross removed from the water tower in Alsip, Illinois, and replaced with a "holiday tree." The article quotes other sources to document such actions are taking place across the nation.

> **The Moral Revolution in Full View**
>
> (ChristianPost.com, January 21, 2011)—A couple in England were found guilty of discrimination because they rented rooms in their small hotel only to married couples. The ruling was based on the new legal foundation that judicial law can no longer accommodate Judaic-Christian beliefs.

> **Younger Generation More Prone to Immoral Behavior, Survey Finds**
>
> (ChristianPost.com, August 26, 2008)—The article states: "The younger generation—known as Mosaics—was nine times more likely than Boomers to have engaged in sex outside of marriage (38 percent vs. 4 percent), six times more likely to have lied (37 percent vs. 6 percent), nearly three times more likely to have gotten drunk (25 percent vs. 9 percent), and twice as likely as Boomers to have watched pornography (33 percent vs. 16 percent)." The decline of those under twenty-two years of age can be traced to the removal of prayer and Bible reading from the public school system in 1963.

> **College: Students Can't Sell "Christmas" Trees**
>
> (blog by Todd Starnes, November 27, 2012)—A North Carolina college violates the First Amendment for not allowing students to use the word "Christmas."

> **Atheists Want Cross Removed from 9/11 World Trade Center Museum**
>
> (ChristianPost.com, July 26, 2011)—The cross the atheists wanted removed from the museum was two iron beams

welded together by intense heat in the remains of the World Trade Center.

> **Are Today's Baby Names Abandoning Bible?**
> (WorldNetDaily.com, December 29, 2012)—In A.D. 2000, thirteen years ago, six out of ten babies born were given Bible names. In 2012, only three out of every ten boys born were given Bible names. Going back to 1960, eight out of ten boys born were given Bible names. There has also been a corresponding reduction in giving Bible names to girl babies. This is an evident proof of the declining influence of the Christian faith in the United States due to Christian cleansing.

> **The NAACP's attack on the Grahams**
> (OneNewsNow.com, November 5, 2012)—The NAACP, in a seven-page letter, accused the Billy Graham Ministry of arousing "unwarranted suspicions" by encouraging Christians to vote according to "their values." The NAACP did not reference their own obvious backing of President Obama.

> **Are Americans Getting Comfortable with Immorality?**
> (ChristianPost.com, May 27, 2011)—A Gallup poll indicates that the majority of U.S. citizens believe that the moral condition of the nation is getting worse. One of the reasons indicated in the article was the increasing pornographic content or references in television shows. Richard Land, president of the Ethics and Religious Commission, stated that those who do not believe that the moral standard of life in the U.S. is getting worse are part of the problem.

> **Christian broadcaster straying from Scripture?**
> (OneNewsNow.com, December 11, 2012)—700 Club host Pat Robertson doubts Genesis chronology of creation.

- **Federal Court Rules Mountaintop Cross Violates Constitution**

  (ABCNews.com, January 4, 2011)—Just another example of "Christian cleansing" in America.

- **Catholic Leader Banned from NYC "Piss Christ" Exhibit**

  (FoxNews.com, September 28, 2012)—A New York gallery refused entrance of an advocacy group to view a vulgar exhibit of Jesus on the cross submerged in the urine of artist Andres Serrano.

- **Colorado and Washington State Approving the Growing, Possession, and Use of Marijuana for Any Purpose**

  (CNN, November 7, 2012)—Several states have voted for the use of marijuana for medical purposes, but now several other states are considering following the examples of Colorado and Washington State. The statistics of the detrimental effect of student users of this drug, as well as traffic accident statistics, are well documented. The examples set by these two states will be followed by others, possibly or probably making allowances for the legal use of hard drugs for all purposes. This again illustrates the declining influence of the church in civil matters.

- **Growing Intolerance for Christianity in U.S.**

  (ChristianPost.com, April 6, 2011)—This news article documents a long list of national or local discriminations against traditional Christian beliefs and practices dating back to 1776. Some of the more current examples given are as follows:

  » The Supreme Court determining to exclude anyone who prays in Jesus' name from a rotation of officials who open city business meetings.

» The removal of U.S. military chaplain Gordon Klingen-schmitt, over the issue of praying in Jesus' name.

» UCLA's prohibiting a graduating student from thanking her "Lord and Saviour Jesus Christ" in her graduation speech.

> **Elimination of Charitable Deductions May Harm Middle Class**

(ChristianPost.com, December 3, 2012)—The elimination of charitable contributions, including tithes or contributions to churches and other Christian organizations, would result in the closing of many organizations, resulting in a further decline of the influence of the Bible on American life.

> **Why One Poll Says 45% Would Rather Skip Christmas**

(CNBC.com, November 19, 2012)—Out of 1,000 U.S. citizens surveyed, 450 said they would like to see Christmas abolished, not only for financial reasons but also that the birth of Jesus Christ means nothing to them.

> **The TV elite "assume Christians are lunatics"**

(*London Telegraph*, September 13, 2012)—Most, including Christians, watch television several hours a day. Television has replaced the daily newspaper, magazines, and radio news broadcasts as the primary source for information and entertainment. It has been reported that only eight out of every one hundred TV program hosts, entertainers, commentators, or news reporters and analysts have ever been inside a church. Yet they have largely replaced other news sources and even church pastors in giving opinions on marriage, homosexuality, and other related moral standards. Although there may be a few Christian-produced programs on TV, television is given credit by many for being the major factor in the decreasing of Christian influence in the United States, as well as other countries.

> **Santa Monica City Nixes Decades-Old Nativity Scene**
> (CBN.com, November 21, 2012)—The sixty-year-old nativity scene was removed as city authorities caved in to pressure from atheist protesters. This is another example of the Christian cleansing of America.

> **Did Jesus have a wife?**
> (WashingtonPost.com, September 18, 2012)—Matthew, Mark, Luke, John, and Paul did not mention that Jesus had a wife or that He was even betrothed to be married, as was the Jewish custom. This is evidently another attempt to discredit Jesus as the Messiah.

> **Seniors decry ban on Christmas tree in their complex in Newhall**
> (*LA Daily News,* December 12, 2012)—The JP Partners Group, which owns apartment buildings in California, Colorado, and Oklahoma, demanded that trees as a religious symbol were to be removed in all communal areas.

> **Kansas governor criticized for speaking at religious event**
> (*Kansas City Star,* December 9, 2012)—Kansas governor Stan Brownback spoke at a Christian meeting in Topeka, gave his salvation testimony, and prayed for the forgiveness of his sins and the sins of others, for which he was criticized by Americans United for Separation of Church and State.

> **Christian Population Declines in the Holy Land**
> (NewsMax.com, November 12, 2006)—This article reports that the Christian population is declining not only in Israel,

but throughout the Muslim nations of the Middle East. The Christian Coptic church in Egypt has all but been wiped out. The following news items indicate this is a worldwide warning of things to come.

» *Persecution of Christians on Rise—in U.S.* (wnd.com, September 17, 2012): Michael Carl, a veteran and pastor, in this article says that he has never seen this level of Christian persecution in the U.S. in his life. He also quotes another Christian pastor, [Shackleford], who says: "There are children being prohibited from writing Merry Christmas to the soldiers, senior citizens being banned from praying over their meals in the Senior Center, the VA banning the mention of God in military funerals, numerous attempts to have veterans' memorials torn down if they have any religious symbols such as a cross, and I could go on and on."

» *Franklin Graham: World's Christians in Grave Danger* (NewsMax.com, March 18, 2011): "The Muslim Brotherhood, with the complicity of the Obama administration, has infiltrated the U.S. government at the highest levels and is influencing American policy that leaves the world's Christians in grave danger, warns internationally known evangelist Franklin Graham. 'The Muslim Brotherhood is very strong and active here in our country,' Graham tells Newsmax. 'We have these people advising our military and State Department. We've brought in Muslims to tell us how to make policy toward Muslim countries. It's like a farmer asking a fox, "How do I protect my hen house?"' That same Muslim Brotherhood is fomenting much of the rebellion and the deteriorating social order roiling the Middle East, forcing millions of Christians to flee for their lives, says Graham, son of beloved evangelist Dr. Billy Graham, and founder of The Samaritan's Purse international charity. Asked if President Barack Obama was doing enough to protect Christians at home and abroad, Graham says, 'No. If anything it's the opposite. Muslims are protected more in this country than Christians are,' he says. 'The president has made many statements but he doesn't back them up. We have to do more to protect the Christians in the Muslim world. Their lives are in danger.'"

The preceding volume of news headlines and stories, the majority being dated between 2010 and 2012, prove without any reasonable doubt that general church membership is in decline, as well as Christian influence in the political, educational, and civic organizations and people of our nation.

Again we reference Jesus' warning that when He returned that the Christian faith would be declining or barely evident. So, what can be done to reverse the Christian cleansing of our beloved nation? Christians must reject the news media propaganda that the church and Christians have no business in addressing moral and civic problems on a local, state, or national level. Every pastor should begin to inform their congregations that Christian cleansing is sweeping America, and then confront them with this challenge.

In the rest of this book we are going to look more closely at where Christian cleansing is happening and what we must do to confront it.

Chapter 1

Christian Cleansing by the U.S. Government

According to the Bible, government is an institution of God for protecting the innocent and prosecuting the guilty, or as we read in Genesis 9:6: "Whoso sheddeth man's blood, by man shall his blood be shed. ..."

There is a misconception today within Christendom in the United States that church and state must be kept separate, and to speak or advocate good government along biblical principles means they will lose their 501(c)3 status, meaning loss of tax exemptions and other benefits. As I understand it, to this time no church or Christian organization has lost their 501(c)3 status with the government for discussing or presenting information about the moral and spiritual qualities of candidates or political parties. Of course, it is in the interest of kings, presidents, and all appointed or elected government officials to take God out of government. This gives them the option or privilege to lie, cheat, make false promises, steal, and persecute those under their authority.

Paul wrote to the church at Corinth: "... where the Spirit of the Lord is, there is liberty" (2 Corinthians 3:17). I participated in five missions in Russia where no Bible had been printed since 1917. The people of Russia were under a despotic, godless government where some 100 million had been killed, and those that lived were under cruel persecution. We went on five missions and tied up towns everywhere because millions came to get a Bible.

In 1965, Zhou En-lai convinced Mao Tse-tung that the reason his policies were failing was because of capitalists and Christians. What followed was the Cultural Revolution in which 100 million were killed. I went to China in 1978 after the trial of the Gang of Four, the last vestige of the Mao government. I helped to start the Underground Church, which today claims 140 million Chinese Christians.

In ancient Israel, a government of godly judges went from town to town to judge and settle problems between the people. But when the people became apathetic and weary of the responsibilities to maintain this judicial order, they cried for a king. The kings put more and more into government services, raised their taxes, and started wars. The nation became weaker, both financially and militarily, until it was overrun by Babylon. Such is the order of the downfall of nations when God is removed from government. Where the Spirit of God is, there is liberty. When rulers and people ignore this basic precept, wars, high taxes, increase of government payrolls, and, finally, bankruptcy, poverty, and being taken over by other nations either by military conquest or immigration are the result.

George Washington said to the Constitutional Convention delegates, "Let us raise a standard to which the wise and honest can repair; the rest is in the hands of God."

John Adams said, "Our Constitution was made only for a moral and religious people. It is wholly inadequate to the government of any other."

Samuel Adams said, "The sum of all is, if we would most truly enjoy the gift of Heaven, let us become a virtuous people; then shall we both deserve and enjoy it."

George Washington also said, "Of all the dispositions and habits which lead to political prosperity, religion and morality are indispensable supports. It is impossible to rightly govern the world without God and the Bible."

Thomas Jefferson said, "All tyranny needs to gain a foothold is for people of good conscience to remain silent."

The Declaration of Independence states: "We hold these truths to be self-evident, that all men are created equal, that they are endowed by their Creator with certain unalienable rights. ..."

The founding fathers of our nation stated without qualification that where the Spirit of God is, there is liberty; where is no Spirit of God, there is tyranny. The problem is not the institution of government, but rather the man or men in the administration of government. The prophetic and historic course of government is explained in 1 Samuel 8:10–18:

> And Samuel told all the words of the LORD unto the people that asked of him a king. And he said, This will be the manner of the king that shall reign over you: He will take your sons, and appoint them for himself, for his chariots, and to be his horsemen; and some shall run before his chariots. And he will appoint him captains over thousands, and captains over fifties; and will set them to ear his ground, and to reap his harvest,

and to make his instruments of war, and instruments of his chariots. And he will take your daughters to be confectionaries, and to be cooks, and to be bakers. And he will take your fields, and your vineyards, and your oliveyards, even the best of them, and give them to his servants. And he will take the tenth of your seed, and of your vineyards, and give to his officers, and to his servants. And he will take your menservants, and your maidservants, and your goodliest young men, and your asses, and put them to his work. He will take the tenth of your sheep: and ye shall be his servants. And ye shall cry out in that day because of your king which ye shall have chosen you; and the LORD will not hear you in that day.

The warning that Samuel gave Israel about the growth and evils of government was fulfilled:

And he said unto them, What counsel give ye that we may answer this people, who have spoken to me, saying, Make the yoke which thy father did put upon us lighter? And the young men that were grown up with him spake unto him, saying, Thus shalt thou speak unto this people that spake unto thee, saying, Thy father made our yoke heavy, but make thou it lighter unto us; thus shalt thou say unto them, My little finger shall be thicker than my father's loins. And now whereas my father did lade you with a heavy yoke, I will add to your yoke: my father hath chastised you with whips, but I will chastise you with scorpions.   —1 Kings 12:9–11

Considering the lessons of history, our founding fathers constructed a government with checks and balances, dividing governmental authority into three separate and distinct parts—executive, legislative, and judicial—with each section having supervisory authority over the other two branches. Even so, George Washington said that if this was insufficient to control government, then the people had the authority to vote the autocrats out of office: *"The power under the Constitution will always be in the people.* It is entrusted for certain defined purposes, and for a certain limited period, to representatives of their own choosing; and whenever it is executed contrary to their interest, or not agreeable to their wishes, their servants can, and undoubtedly will, be recalled."

It is obvious that the main concern of our founding fathers was shepherding the new nation in a governmental system that in years to come would not be responsible to the will of the majority. "If angels were to govern men, neither external nor internal controls on government would be necessary. In framing a government which is to be administered by men over men, the great difficulty lies in this: you must first enable the government to control the governed; and in the next place oblige it to control itself" (*The Federalist Papers: Essays by Alexander Hamilton, John Jay, and James Madison*).

Something that was not envisioned by the framers of our Constitution in 1776 was the growth of the nation into many more states in different geological sections of the continent, resulting in different economic, political, and even racial differences. Therefore, in 1861 what was known as the American Civil War—a war between the states over equal states' rights—erupted. Even so, the nation with its republican form of government survived during the ensuing traumatic years.

However, since 1865 the nation has doubled in size and population. The nation has also been involved in two world wars, gone through the Great Depression of the 1930s, and in recent years been subjected to massive immigration—with lax or no citizenship requirements—by millions who have come from nations with different forms of government, religions, and economic conditions. King David was faced with a similar problem, and the Lord told him to wait until he heard a rustling in the mulberry tree, and then chase them back to their own country. What we may need in our nation is a rustling of the mulberry tree.

In a communist-governed nation, everything produced or earned is controlled by the government, and then the government determines the "fair share" that should be returned to each citizen. Under this system, everybody works for the government.

One of the greatest books ever produced on God, government, and the law was written in 1849 by Frederic Bastiat, a member of the French parliament. The book, entitled *The Law,* involves the perversion of the power of government to take from citizens who have and give it to citizens who do not have in order to perpetuate their political power and offices. Bastiat called this system political robbery or legal plunder. His thesis also presents a basic political truth that if a politician in office, or one running for office, can promise fifty-one percent of the people that he will take money from the other forty-nine percent and give it to them, he can perpetuate his job and perhaps become a dictator.

For whatever purpose or reason, this process began in earnest in the administration of Franklin D. Roosevelt (referred to as the New Deal). This process via taxation and government subsidies has continued and expanded in following subsequent administrations, the present administration of Barack Obama being no exception … and possibly the guiltiest. Current reports as of January 2013 indicate that 45 million Americans participate in the government food stamp program, and considering all federally-funded aid or pension programs, over half of the U.S. population are the recipients of "legal plunder."

To illustrate and document the destined course of the government of the United States, from 1776 to 2013, we present the following:

> **U.S.-Mexico Pact Revealed: Billions to Non-Citizens**
> (NewsMax.com, January 5, 2007)—The state of Texas has a very large immigration from Mexico. President George W. Bush, seemingly in order to enhance his political favor in his own state, used legal plunder to send billions of dollars to claimants in Mexico under the U.S.-Mexico Social Security Totalization Agreement. This agreement, signed in 2004, may have helped him get the Hispanic vote when running for president. This questionable agreement may be one reason why the U.S. Social Security program is in financial trouble.

> **U.S. Postal Service on a "Tightrope" Lost $15.9 Billion**
> (Bloomberg.com, November 15, 2012)—Postage rates have increased yearly since A.D. 2000, yet the department suffers a huge yearly deficit. While the U.S. Postal Service does a good job in a tremendous public-service need, many incompetents and immigrants are hired who are actually detrimental. At Southwest Radio Church we had to send out our mail with a return of address of simply "SWRC" rather than using our name because our mail was being thrown away. Legal plun-

der for political purposes is active in all U.S. government departments.

> **Homeland Security graduates first Corps of Homeland Youth**
> (e-mail received from a listener, October 30, 2012)—Soon after President Obama was elected in 2008, he promised a FEMA corps larger than state militias or the U.S. Army. According to the article, this "standing army of government youth will be paid for full-time service." Why would the president need his own army? Comparisons are being made between this FEMA army and the Brown Shirts of Hitler and the army of Mao Tse-tung that killed some 100 million in the Cultural Revolution between 1965 and 1975.

> **Drones at home raise fear of surveillance society**
> (Associated Press, June 23, 2012)—This article reports the concern of many Americans that within ten years drones will be flying constantly over every city, giving Washington complete control over traffic, housing, and any possible resistance to federal authority.

> **Victory puts Obama in position to expand government's reach**
> (Reuters.com, November 7, 2012)—This British source thinks that President Obama will again increase the power and outreach of the executive branch of government in the area of medical service, immigration, and governmental activism.

> **Senate-Passed Deal Means Higher Tax on 77 Percent of Households**
> (Bloomberg.com, January 1, 2013)—The average increase per household in 2013 will be $1,635.

> **Student sues over "locator" chips**
>
> (Associated Press, November 27, 2012)—Under the present administration of President Obama, the use of the microchip has become more prevalent. The headline above references a student in the San Antonio school system who refused to have a chip in her identification card. Often referenced is the use of a microchip implanted in each citizen under Obamacare to be able to get medical care at all. It is claimed that under a national health program the microchip for identification and medical records would be necessary. According to the Book of Revelation, during the Tribulation unless a person has the "mark and number" of the Antichrist, they will not be able to buy or sell, and probably not get medical care. This would give the government a tremendous weapon for mass control.

> **Election Fraud? Barack Obama Won More Than 99 Percent of the Vote in More Than 100 Ohio Precincts**
>
> (MarketDailyNews.com, November 12, 2012)—In the 2012 presidential election, there were also a large number of precincts in Pennsylvania reporting that the Republican candidate did not receive a single vote. Seasoned news analysts concluded that this was impossible. There were also reports that in some precincts, voters could not get the computerized voting units to register a vote for the Republican candidate. If such reports have a measure of credibility, then we might as well destroy our Constitution and abolish voting. It appears odd.

> **Legalize Drugs, But Criminalize Guns: Stats Show Firearms Kill Fewer Americans**
>
> (CNS.com, December 20, 2012)—Although statistics prove

that marijuana users in school make lower grades and that its use causes traffic accidents, Washington and Colorado voted to make this drug legal for any use, including "entertainment." Various sources indicate that President Obama used drugs as late as 1999. He also used his authority as president to remove federal protection of the Defense of Marriage Act.

> **White House "secede" petitions reach 675,000 signatures, 50-state participation**
> (DailyCaller.com, November 14, 2012)—Many citizens were concerned about voting irregularities and the result of the presidential election.

> **Ranchers, farmers brace for "death tax" impact**
> (FoxNews.com, November 16, 2012)—Kevin Kesler inherited a ranch and is being called upon to pay more than $13 million in inheritance taxes. And now the president wants to increase inheritance and capital gains taxes to help offset the $6 trillion deficit accrued during the first four years of his administration.

> **5.4 Million Join Disability Rolls Under Obama**
> (Investors.com, April 20, 2012)—This means that millions can now join the disability rolls—and get paid for the rest of their lives—without working. This is in addition to the 45 million on food stamps.

> **Obama Administration Says It Talked With Muslim Brotherhood to Promote Small Business**
> (CNS.com, April 23, 2012)—The Muslim Brotherhood promotes a worldwide Islamic movement, as indicated in the Koran, to prepare the world for an Islamic conquest and the return of the Mahdi to kill everyone who is not a Mus-

lim. Many believe President Obama is more Muslim than Christian.

> **It's All Your Money: Foreign Aid to Muslim/Arab Nations**
(FoxNews.com, May 24, 2011)—Arab and Muslim nations receive as much as $40 million a year each from U.S. foreign aid, yet vote for the U.S. position in the U.N. only eighteen percent of the time.

> **Gallup: Nearly 7 Out of 10 Americans Are Dissatisfied With the Size and Power of Government—and with Nation's Moral Climate**
(CNS.com, February 7, 2011)—In 2001, a Gallup poll indicated that sixty-eight percent of Americans were satisfied with our form of government and moral standards. Today, only forty-two percent said they were satisfied with our government and moral condition.

> **Pentagon wants to know: "Did Jesus die for Klingons too?"**
(WashingtonTimes.com, November 15, 2012)—Senator Tom Coburn (R-OK) contends that the Pentagon is spending much of its $600 billion budget on stupid projects like wanting to know if aliens are discovered living on other planets if the message of salvation in Jesus Christ would apply to them.

> **Hidden Government Scanners Will Instantly Know Everything About You From 164 Feet Away**
(gizmodo.com, July 12, 2012)—A report concerning Homeland Security's increased use of laser scanners in public places and how they will know everything about you that the agency would need or want to know.

> **Obama's America Will Become Detroit**
(CNS.com, December 12, 2012)—In Detroit, President Obama

referenced federal aid to General Motors to save the company, and indicated that he would make the United States another Detroit. But the article presents the following statistics:

» In 1950 Detroit's population was 1,845,568. Today it is 708,586.

» Of the present population, less than half have a job.

» Of those who are employed, 15.3 percent work for the government.

» 34.5 percent of the population of Detroit gets food stamps from the government.

» Only 9.2 percent of the households in Detroit are married couples with children.

» 75.4 percent of the babies born in Detroit are born to unmarried women.

» There are 99,072 vacant housing units in Detroit.

» Of school children in Detroit, only seven percent are proficient at grade level reading, and only four percent are proficient at grade level math.

These statistics again raise the question: Do government subsidies really help, or do they just make the poor poorer as they look to the government rather than trying to help themselves.

> **Surveillance Is on the Rise**

(Google.com, November 14, 2012)—Google reports that requests from the U.S. government for specific information has doubled in 2012 over 2011.

> **Obama Administration: We Can and Will Force Christians to Act Against Their Faith**

(CNS.com, December 29, 2012)—The Obama administration

has judged that Hobby Lobby of Oklahoma City must pay $1.3 million a day in fines for failing to provide emergency contraception in their health plans. This will also apply to all churches and Christian organizations, which is against the free exercise of religion as set forth in our Constitution.

> **75% of New Jobs Created in Last 5 Months Are in Government**
> (CNS.com, December 7, 2012)—A greater percentage being employed by the government is one of the surest signs that within a few years, perhaps four, the U.S. will be a communist nation like Russia and China were. This probably also means the church and Christians will be persecuted as they were in those two nations.

> **Hindu, Buddhist win first-time seats**
> (WashingtonTimes.com, November 18, 2012)—Hawaii elects one Hindu and one Buddhist to Congress. This report by the Pew Forum indicates a steady reduction of Protestant members of Congress over the past fifty years.

> **FBI wants palm prints, eye scans, tattoo mapping**
> (CNN.com, February 5, 2008)—The article states that the FBI is creating a massive database on people's physical characteristics for possible future identification purposes. Concern is expressed about private and personal liberty.

> **"Big Brother" plan for police to use new road cameras**
> (Guardian.co.uk, July 18, 2007)—The travels of every American car on the highways can be traced and given to the police if needed.

> **FAQ: How Real ID will affect you**
> (CNET [news.com], May 6, 2005)—The House of Representa-

tives has approved $82 million for an electronic ID card for every American. Although this has been approved, it is not being enforced at this time.

> **Report: Enough Spent on Welfare Programs in 2011 to Write Every Poor Household a $59,523 Check**
> (CNS.com, October 30, 2012)—$1 trillion was spent on welfare programs by the federal government in 2011 for 16 million families earning below $23,000 a year.

> **Senate bill rewrite lets feds read your e-mail without warrants**
> (CNET [news.com], November 20, 2012)—This new law passed by Congress will permit any or all twenty-two government agencies access your e-mail without a warrant. E-mail is, or has become, the most common method of correspondence between Americans, giving the government the right to know what every American is, or is not, doing.

> **Social Security Ran $47.8B Deficit in FY2012; Disabled Workers Hit New Record in December: 8,827,795**
> (CNS.com, December 26, 2012)—The average increase in Social Security pay deduction in 2013 will be $1,000. Christian cleansing, or Christian fleecing of Americans?

> **One Small Step for Hand …**
> (bmezine.com, May 3, 2012)—An eight-page presentation on the microchipping of the hand for future identification purposes in connection with government services, employment, or government programs like Medicare.

> **Welfare hasn't reduced poverty, says expert**
> (OneNewsNow.com, September 19, 2012)—President Lyndon B. Johnson promoted the idea that the poor and unemployed

can be encouraged and given the means to better themselves. According to the article, it has not helped. The Apostle Paul warned the churches about helping those who were able to work.

> **Govt "creating vast domestic snooping machine"**
> (Breitbart.com, December 20, 2007)—Due to concerns about foreign terrorists within the American workforce and general population, the FBI is using local law enforcement agencies to build a file on millions of Americans for further use by Homeland Security.

> **Big Brother's Listening**
> (TheDaily.com, December 11, 2012)—The federal government, according to the article, is quietly installing microphones in every public bus, reportedly for security reasons.

> **Intelligence community: U.S. out as sole superpower by 2030**
> (politico.com, December 10, 2012)—An intelligence report from Global Trends projects that by 2030 China will be the world's superpower and the U.S. will fall economically and military-wise to the level of many other nations.

> **... Tenth most popular Christmas list request for children**
> (*London Telegraph*, December 26, 2012)—One of the most frequent Christmas gifts that children asked for during the 2012 Christmas season was simply "a dad."

> **USA becomes Food Stamp Nation, but is it sustainable?**
> (Yahoo.com, August 23, 2011)—This news item reports that in August of 2011, there were 46 million U.S. citizens on food stamps. Since the date of this report, the number on food stamps has increased exponentially.

> **Obama Vows More Tax Increases**
> (WhiteHouseDossier.com, January 2, 2013)—According to Winston Churchill, "For a nation to tax itself into prosperity is like a man standing in a bucket trying to lift himself with the handle."

> **Obama urging state lawmakers to legalize gay marriage in Illinois**
> (SunTimes.com, December 29, 2012)—President Obama receives much of his financial support from homosexuals for his efforts to get gay marriage legalized in every state.

We began this chapter by referencing the Apostle Paul's advice to the Christians at Corinth: "… where the Spirit of the Lord is, there is liberty" (2 Corinthians 3:17). Let us all pray for a revival within our churches and a return to the plain Gospel message of the Bible. In order to retain a free and prosperous America, we must return the Spirit of the Lord to our country.

Chapter 2

The President

The president of the United States is often referred to as the "chief executive." The president conducts the affairs of state mainly through presidential assistants, or as President Obama has termed them, "czars"—a Russian communist official.

After party runoffs, usually two candidates—one from the Republican Party and one from the Democratic Party—present to the nation each party's plans that will supposedly improve the social, economic, and military security of the nation. The president must get his promised programs mainly through Congress in order for them to become the law of the land. He can also supplement his authority through the use of presidential directives, or executive orders.

One of the most admirable accomplishments of a president is the ability to inspire, encourage, and give confidence to the people of his abilities to lead them in every phase of national life. Presidents who were outstanding in this respect were George Washington, Abraham Lincoln, Theodore Roosevelt, and Ronald Reagan.

Franklin D. Roosevelt has been the only president to be elected for three terms. Many thought he was too socialistic and nearly communistic in his economic policies. However, he must be given credit for taking the nation through the Great Depression of the 1930s. Also, during his second term, the United States entered World War II, and over 16 million men and women were enlisted in the Army, Navy, and Air Corps. This meant producing thousands of tanks; thousands of airplanes; millions of rifles; millions of shoes, pants, shirts; millions of tons of ammunition, food, and transportation for this massive force. It seems unlikely that such a massive accomplishment could be done today, even though the population has increased from 200 million to over 300 million.

While Ulysses S. Grant and Dwight D. Eisenhower were great generals, they did not make great presidents. Yet, Ronald Reagan, a movie actor, became one of the most loved and admired presidents. Most Christians would prefer to have a dedicated and fundamental Christian as president, but of recent vintage, both Jimmy Carter and Bill Clinton were members of Southern Baptist churches. Carter became one of our more disappointing presidents, and Clinton through his economic policies caused loans to be given to millions for expensive housing for which they could not pay. This caused the housing crash of 2008, with most homeowners losing forty percent of their real estate value. Clinton was also impeached for having sex with an aide in the Oval Office of the White House and then lying about it. While the man (or woman) in the White House is a president, not a pastor, in keeping with our national and founding history, to keep the United States the United States, it is always preferable to have a person of Christian faith to lead our country. The church affiliations of our forty-four presidents is as follows:

- **Baptist**
  - Warren Harding
  - Harry Truman (Southern Baptist)
  - Jimmy Carter (former Southern Baptist)
  - Bill Clinton (former Southern Baptist)

- **Congregationalist**
  - Calvin Coolidge
  - John Adams (later Unitarian)

- **Disciples of Christ**
  - James Garfield
  - Lyndon Johnson
  - Ronald Reagan (also Presbyterian)

- **Dutch Reformed**
  - Martin Van Buren
  - Theodore Roosevelt

- **Episcopalian**
  - George Washington
  - James Madison
  - James Monroe
  - William Henry Harrison
  - John Tyler
  - Zachary Taylor
  - Franklin Pierce
  - Chester A. Arthur
  - Franklin D. Roosevelt
  - Gerald Ford
  - George H. W. Bush
  - George W. Bush (later Methodist)

> **Methodist**
>> James Polk (originally Presbyterian)
>> Ulysses S. Grant (allegedly; his theology is unknown)
>> William McKinley
>> George W. Bush (originally Episcopalian)

> **Presbyterian**
>> Andrew Jackson
>> James Polk (later Methodist)
>> James Buchanan
>> Grover Cleveland
>> Benjamin Harrison
>> Woodrow Wilson
>> Dwight D. Eisenhower
>> Ronald Reagan (also Disciples of Christ)

> **Quaker**
>> Herbert Hoover
>> Richard Nixon

> **Roman Catholic**
>> John F. Kennedy

> **Unitarian**
>> John Adams
>> John Quincy Adams
>> Millard Fillmore
>> William Howard Taft

> **United Church of Christ**
>> Barack Obama (later no affiliation)

> **No denominational affiliation**
>> Thomas Jefferson
>> Abraham Lincoln

- » Andrew Johnson
- » Ulysses S. Grant
- » Rutherford Hayes
- » Barack Obama (previously United Church of Christ)

Our last president, Barack Obama, did belong to a church, but his former pastor said that he joined their church for political reasons, that he and his wife were really not church people. There have been considerable opinions from those who follow President Obama's off duties, including golf, that he is more a Muslim than a Christian. As indicated now in some reports, he is considered an atheist. President Obama's efforts on behalf of anti-Christian conduct, morals, and the family places him high on the list of those who are in the "Christian cleansing" of the United States.

We read in 2 Corinthians 3:17, ". . . where the Spirit of the Lord is, there is liberty." World history covering the past two thousand years will prove without exception that where Christian faith in Jesus Christ is preached and accepted by the citizenry, freedom always follows: freedom of worship; freedom of speech; freedom of commerce and labor; freedom of the family unit from fear. To again enslave a nation in the course of brutal dictators, the Gospel of Jesus Christ as proclaimed by the voice of Christians, with the support of the church, must be silenced. Before men and women of any nation are forced to accept a totalitarian dictatorship, they must turn from God before accepting a godless dictatorship. There must be a "cleansing" of that nation of any truth about God or the Bible. Karl Marx, the godfather of communism, boasted that he would throw his glove in the face of God and stroll through the world a creator.

In Russia, children were asked to pray to God for a cookie. When they lifted their heads, there was no cookie. Then they were told to pray to Stalin for a cookie. While their heads were bowed, the teacher would place a cookie on their desks. They were trained at an early age to look to government rather than God for help.

In Russia from 1918 to 1989, the only religious authority recognized was the Russian Orthodox Church, which was in league with the Communist Party. Churches were closed, all Bibles were confiscated and burned, approximately 80 million people were killed, and countless others were imprisoned and tortured. The anti-Christian cleansing process in Russia made possible the cruelest, most inhuman political system ever known.

When the Iron Curtain finally parted in 1989, I personally led Bible tours to Russia each year with Dr. Robert Lindsted. The thirst for God's Word was almost unbelievable. We tied up hundreds of towns with Russians coming by the millions to get a Bible.

In 1975, Zhou En-lai convinced Mao that in order for his communist programs to succeed, he would first have to cleanse China of all capitalists and religionists. This began one of the most horrible waves of murder and terror ever known. It was called the "Cultural Revolution." The remaining churches were burned, and thousands of Chinese clergy were starved to death in labor communes. The total number killed by the Red Guard in the ten-year period from 1965 to 1975 has been estimated at 100 million. After Mao's death in 1976, the bloody Cultural Revolution subsided, and after the trial of the Gang of Four, a few state-controlled churches began to open. I was at the first service of the Moen church in Shanghai after the Cultural Revolution. Later, joining with Dr. Lindsted and others, we smuggled millions of Bibles into

China. Non-government approved churches, called Underground Churches, began to spread through China. My booklet, known as *The Happiness Story,* which I wrote in 1980, continues to be published in Hong Kong and remains the chief outreach item used by the Underground Church today. It is estimated the number of Christians in the Underground Church in China exceeds 40 million.

However, it should be noted that before anti-God, inhuman dictatorship could be imposed on China and Russia, a period of so-called Christian cleansing had to occur. A similar period of Christian cleansing is now taking place in the United States.

It is well known that school activities and textbooks are now rigidly monitored and policed by anti-Christian government officials and departments to delete any reference to God or our Christian heritage. Scripture references and devotionals that were once welcomed in schools are now forbidden. Christians at one time could rent school buildings or other government facilities for Christian activities, and that is now forbidden. Any scriptural texts on school buildings, government sites, or open road signs are now forbidden.

Sodomy was the sin that destroyed Sodom and Gomorrah, but now sodomy (homosexuality) is no longer considered a sin. Sodomites are welcomed into our Armed Services and same-sex marriages are now accepted as a legal relationship by our president and many states. Several denominations, like the Presbyterian Church, no longer consider sodomy a sin and are welcoming homosexuals into their pulpits.

The passage of the Obama Healthcare Act will force every citizen to look to the government for healthcare. More and more

Christians will look to Washington for help in time of need rather than praying to God for help. Already, millions are looking to Washington for Social Security payments, food stamps, Aid for Dependent Children, food and housing subsidies, local earmarks, dozens of grants for education, and dozens more for other needs and projects. Now they must look to Washington for healthcare. In the future, if you do not do what the government dictates, you may not get healthcare.

Now, even memorials that have any reference to God or the Bible, including war memorials, along highways or prominent places are being dismantled. The political propaganda mind-set was that the less the citizenry looked to God for help, the more they would look to the government.

I believed that the Christians in this nation would rise up in righteous anger, or the pastors would unite in protest, but neither has happened. Most now fear what the government may do,instead of what God may do.

According to Ussher, in 1897 B.C., there was a gigantic explosion on the Syrian-African Rift where the cities of Sodom and Gomorrah were located. The explosion created a huge ditch ten miles wide, forty miles long, and sixteen hundred feet deep. It is called now the Dead Sea, where nothing has ever lived. Over and over in the Bible the nations are warned to consider the judgment on Sodom. In Romans 1, the Apostle Paul warned that any nation that allows this sin is worthy of death. We will consider this subject more in the chapter on homosexuality. This chapter is not intended to be a harangue about Mr. Obama, but he is the culmination of the course of the progressive Christian cleansing of America.

The following headline stories relate even more clearly the course of government, including the presidency, on the planned Christian cleansing of America:

> **Election Over, Administration Unleashes New Rules**
> (Associated Press, December 13, 2012)—Planned for months, but waiting until the 2012 election to be put in force, the administration has new strict rules for power plants, Wall Street, and others.

> **Florida nears 1 million permits for concealed weapons**
> (Reuters, December 12, 2012)—More citizens are obtaining guns for self-protection before new regulations restrict gun ownership.

> **Obama condemns rights of Christian military chaplains**
> (Associated Press, January 4, 2013)—In signing the $633 billion bill for the 2013 military budget, the president said he did so with reservations because the bill reserved the right of conscience for military chaplains who did not want to marry two men or two women.

> **White House panic: Corsi book targeted**
> (WorldNetDaily.com, May 19, 2011)—The efforts of the White House to attack charges that Obama is not legally eligible to be president. The response to these charges seems to be that such distractions come from uninformed right-wing kooks. However, qualified experts have testified that the president's so-called birth certificate is made of piecemeal information from several sources; that the name of the hospital listed on the birth certificate is the current name, not the name of the hospital when Mr. Obama was born; and his Social Security

number is that of a young girl who died several decades ago. But no amount of evidence proving Mr. Obama is not qualified to be president will ever be considered by Congress or the Supreme Court for obvious reasons—he is popular with the sub-middle class population; he is half black; and no one in government wants to become involved in what could be an anti-racial controversy.

> **Religious affiliations of Presidents of the United States** (Wikipedia.com)—This article from Wikipedia attempts to explain President Obama's atheistic, non-religious beliefs in the view that several other presidents (including both Lincoln and Washington) could have been atheists, which is the opinion of a Wikipedia contributor. Because of the nature of Wikipedia (a free online encyclopedia that anyone can edit), information thereon must be considered only in conjunction with other documented information. The information on particular people is often entered from questionable sources. For example, the information from Wikipedia has me setting exact dates for Jesus' return, which I never have. I have often referenced the signs of His return, but according to biblical warnings, I have never set a calendar date for His coming.

> **Arpaio: Obama birth record "definitely fraudulent"** (Associated Press, July 18, 2012)—Investigators for Sheriff Joe Arpaio of Maricopa County, Arizona, have concluded that the president's birth certificate is a complete fraud.

> **President daughters now designated "senior staff"** (WorldNetDaily.com, October 4, 2011)—President Obama's two daughters are officially listed as senior assistants to the president so they can join their parents on excursions and

vacations to Africa, Hawaii, and other places, at the taxpayers expense.

> **White House Releases Copy of Long Form of Obama's Birth Certificate from Hawaii**
> (NewsMax.com, April 27, 2011)—Donald Trump challenged President Obama to also release his college transcripts and other related records. The picture of the birth certificate is shown within the quoted article, but was later challenged by other sources as not being authentic.

The importance of the head of government identifying with the nation's history, spiritual or church affiliation, and the basic political form of government is illustrated as a new king, queen, or political head (being a descendant of the former national leaders) is to maintain the same national governmental system. This is why the long genealogical descendants of Jesus Christ are given in Matthew and Luke. A nation cannot have a new head of government who will suddenly change the complete order of government, economics, or even traditional spiritual beliefs and practices overnight. In this regard, considering President Obama's beliefs and historical past, it would seem doubtful that he is qualified to be president of the United States.

> **Black Pastors: Stay Home on Election Day**
> (Associated Press, September 18, 2012)—Many black pastors asked their members to stay home during the November 2012 election rather than vote for a Mormon or a president who approves of homosexual marriage.

> **FBI Asked to Probe Obama "Vote-Changing" Machines**
> (WorldNetDaily.com, November 26, 2012)—A Maryland state

lawmaker has asked for an investigation into reports that some of the voting machines failed to record votes for the Republican candidate, Mitt Romney.

> **Gun Maker's Stock Soars More Than 700% Since Obama's Inauguration in 2009**
> (CNSNews.com, December 18, 2012)—The article suggests the reason for the rush of more Americans to buy guns is lack of confidence or uncertainty as to policies of the Obama administration.

> **Agenda 21: Obama's Plan for America**
> (DickMorris.com, October 9, 2012)—Agenda 21 is a United Nations program advocating U.N. control over sustainable development in relation to gas, air, ground, forests, energy, etc. Obama is in favor of placing U.N. control over practically everything that U.S. citizens do or don't do.

> **It's All Your Money: Foreign Aid to Muslim/Arab nations**
> (FoxNews.com, May 24, 2011)—This article states without qualification that two-thirds of our huge foreign aid budget goes to Arab/Muslim nations, enemies of Israel whose votes in the United Nations are consistently against U.S. interests. Foreign aid is given at the request of the president.

> **Executive Order: National Defense Resources Preparedness**
> (Whitehouse.gov via e-mail, March 6, 2012)—The commentary attached to this eight-page executive order contends that by this order, President Obama has made himself a dictator.

> **Shift on Executive Power Lets Obama Bypass Rivals**
> (*New York Times,* April 23, 2012)—An editorial by Charlie Savage charges that the president is exceeding executive powers of the office in withdrawing legal recognition of the

Defense of Marriage Act to more quickly promote same-sex marriage.

> **Odd? Romney Got ZERO Votes in 59 Precincts in Philly, and 9 Precincts in Ohio**
> (TheBlaze.com, November 12, 2012)—Other reports indicate that in over 100 precincts President Obama received 99 percent of the votes. Seasoned observers contend that this was an impossibility.

> **Two-thirds of jobs go to immigrants during Obama's four years**
> (*Washington Times,* October 31, 2012)—This report indicates that President Obama favors immigrants, both legal and illegal, more than he does American citizens.

> **Jim Rogers: It's Going To Get Really "Bad After the Election"**
> (MoneyMorning.com, September 11, 2012)—A warning that during the next four years after the 2012 election, Americans must prepare for a financial Armageddon.

> **Obama Has Massive Lead in Global Poll**
> (*The Weekly Standard,* October 23, 2012)—In a poll of over 21,000 foreign citizens, Mitt Romney received only 20 percent of the vote. The obvious indication is that President Obama would make a good international president. He favors foreigners more than he does U.S. citizens.

> **Texas Megachurch Pastor Says Obama Will "Pave Way" for Antichrist**
> (ChristianPost.com, November 8, 2012)—Robert Jeffress, pastor of the First Baptist Church of Dallas, in a sermon just before the election in November 2012, said that if Mr. Obama is re-elected, he will pave the way for the Antichrist. He did

not say that President Obama was the Antichrist, but that he was a forerunner.

> **First Openly Gay Man Chosen as the New White House Social Secretary**
>
> (ABC News, February 25, 2011)—This news item needs no further comment.

> **What? No Easter Greeting**
>
> (blog by Keith Koffler, April 28, 2011)—An observation that President Obama has issued a special notice and declaration for four Muslim holy days, but not one word about Easter and the resurrection of Jesus Christ.

We are sure that President Obama has some commendable attributes and accomplishments in office; otherwise he would not have won in the November 2012 election. Or, it may be as Bastiat wrote in 1849 on his deathbed: It doesn't make any difference what a ruler does as long as he convinces fifty-one percent or more of the people that he can take money from the other forty-nine percent and give it to them. He can rule as he pleases until the forty-nine percent go broke.

Chapter 3

Christian Cleansing in the United States Armed Forces

Perhaps evidence of the "Christian cleansing" of America is more evident in the Armed Forces of the United States than any other segment of government or the civil order. This may be surprising to some, but if the United States is to be destroyed in relation to its laws and government, the military must also be abolished or made of none effect.

No nation has ever maintained its freedom of life, liberty, and the pursuit of happiness by a friendly handshake and open borders with its neighbor nations. We know from Scripture that God divided the nations and set the bounds of their habitation, but it is Satan's plan to create war and disorder to bring about a one-world order over which his king, the Antichrist, will reign and rule.

God gave the descendants of Abraham a plot of land, but no nation has had to fight more to retain their country than Israel. In the Old Testament, we read that in the dozens of wars that Israel had to wage in defense of their country, their prayer would be that God go out with their armies. Faith in swords, guns, bombs, or bullets is not enough. There must also be a faith in God to honor the cause for which a nation may have to enter into armed conflict, and, if the cause is just, to give them the victory.

In the records of the Revolutionary War against England in 1776, the prayers of George Washington and the reliance of the patriots upon God is evident in the letters that the officers and enlisted men wrote home to their loved ones. British loyalists during the American Revolution even referred to a "black robe brigade" when referencing Protestant clergymen, predominantly non-Anglican, that assisted in rallying the populace to take up arms against the crown.

In World War II, churches across the nation had special prayers for the soldiers fighting on foreign fronts, and they did what they could to send encouraging letters and prayers. During World War II, there was a chaplain with every battalion or naval unit. On Sunday, when possible, the bugler would summon church or devotional meetings with the pastor, and the chaplains were always there to counsel with the soldiers about loneliness or concerns about family and loved ones at home. Even in the jungles of New Guinea and the Philippines, one of the most important times was meeting with the chaplain for prayer and spiritual assurance that everything would be all right. Even the commander-in-chief of the Armed Forces of the United States, President Franklin Roosevelt, would always end his national address to the people with prayer and recognition that God is the determining factor in any war.

In the Armed Forces, there is a code of trust and honor from man to man. In the course of all the wars of history, women did not serve except perhaps in a very minor and isolated role. The only time in history that homosexuals served in the army was twenty-two hundred years ago in Alexander's army. Alexander had a regiment of homosexuals called "The Companions," but at least he had sense enough to keep them in a separate unit, away from his regular soldiers.

Most Americans have always been proud of our men in the Armed Services, but recently this has given way to serious concerns over the issue of homosexuals being openly enlisted. It is true that this concern is mainly within the Christian population, but this is also the reason for Christian cleansing from the Atlantic to the Pacific. God's judgment upon Sodom and Gomorrah is mentioned in many scriptures as a warning. God warned time and time again, as Paul referenced in the first chapter of Romans, that if you do this God will forsake you and destroy you like He did Sodom.

The door opening for homosexual enlistment in the Armed Forces began with President Bill Clinton, whose character was demonstrated in his having sex with an aide while in the White House and then lying about it. For this, he was impeached. Nevertheless, he was able to succeed as commander-in-chief of the Armed Forces to obtain entrance in the Army, Navy, Air Force, and Marines for homosexuals, as long as they kept their sexual preference secret.

In World War II, while serving in the South Pacific during the war, a replacement was transferred to our AAA-gun battalion. On his second day it was discovered that he was a homosexual. He was separated in a tent away from the camp. An armed MP stood guard over him until he could be sent back to the States and given a Section 8 discharge for mental illness. In 1943, homosexuality was still considered a mental illness.

In light of today's model of welcoming homosexuals into the Armed Forces, this incident seems rather cruel and homophobic. However, until the election of Mr. Obama, the new commander-in-chief of the Armed Services, this was not an uncommon method of discharging homosexuals from the military. At Valley Forge, when George Washington was in command of the Army, a homosexual was discovered in the ranks. In front of the full regiment in parade dress, the homosexual was presented, and as the drums began to roll, he was marched out from the camp. This incident is the basis for the common expression of disgrace, "being drummed out of the Army."

Today, thousands, and perhaps millions, of homosexuals are joining some branch of our Armed Forces. This is causing concerns by former soldiers and by Christians who are aware of God's judgment against this sin. Today we should be concerned about the revival of military power in the Soviet Union and the growing Chinese army, which is supported by a tremendous, thriving economy. It is my opinion that this places the United States in a dangerous position in the coming decade.

The following headline news stories tell more than I possibly can about the concerns over our Armed Forces and the assault to remove any relevance to our Bible or faith in God that has been a part of our past.

> **Pastor withdrawn from Obama inauguration after sermon on homosexuality surfaces**
  (FoxNews.com, January 10, 2013)—Pastor Louis Giglio of Atlanta was scheduled to give the invocation prayer at the 2013

inauguration of Barack Obama as president for another term. However, his name was withdrawn from that supposed honor when it was discovered in checking his activities (we suppose since birth), that in a 1995 sermon he said that homosexuality was a sin. But God in at least fifty places in His Word has said that homosexuality is not only a sin, but that any nation that goes like Sodom will be destroyed like Sodom.

➤ **"Alarming": 265,000 may leave military if DADT reversed**
(*The Baptist Press,* December 15, 2010)—Senator John McCain, a hero of the Vietnam War, warned about the adverse effect the open enlistment of homosexuals in the Army could have. While this may have been an exaggeration, evidence indicates that more homosexuals, but fewer non-homosexuals, are joining, resulting in an eventual homosexual Army.

➤ **Army Suicides This Year Exceed 2012 Combat Deaths in Afghanistan**
(CNSNews.com, October 23, 2012)—No one in my fifteen hundred-man battalion, or in the First Cavalry Armored Division that I directed artillery for, committed suicide, nor as far as I am aware did anyone in any unit that I knew of commit suicide, even under the most difficult conditions in the South Pacific. This would indicate there is a loss of honor and patriotism in the Armed Forces today.

➤ **Marine Corps Chief: "Distraction" of Gays Serving Openly Could Cost Marines Limbs**
(FoxNews.com, December 14, 2010)—Marine Corps commander General James Amos warned that allowing homosexuals to openly enlist into the Armed Forces would be a major distraction, weakening the fighting efficiency of the Marines.

> **Straight Troops Must Shower With Gays, Says DoD Working Group—"Gay Men Have Learned to Avoid Making Heterosexuals Feel Uncomfortable or Threatened in Situations Such as This"**
> (CNSNews.com, December 18, 2010)—The commander-in-chief of our Army and Navy uses forced examples for all Americans, including Christians, to accept the homosexual lifestyle as normal and acceptable.

> **Christians differ on lifting "don't ask, don't tell"**
> (OneNewsNow.com, November 30, 2010)—This report indicates that only white evangelicals were opposed to the president's plan to open military service to unrestricted enlistment of homosexuals. This was one of the early indications that the United States was becoming another Sodom and Gomorrah.

> **Proposed Army manual tells G.I.s not to insult Taliban, speak up for women**
> (FoxNews.com, December 12, 2012)—This change in Army policy amounts to compromise with evil and wasting lives in Afghanistan.

> **Armed Services Subcommittee Chair: DoD Instructing Military "To Do Things Which Are in Fact Illegal to Do"**
> (CNSNews.com, September 30, 2011)—Armed Services Subcommittee chair, Rep. Todd Akins (R-MO) said:
>
> "One of the things that's increasingly alarming to many Americans is the nature of various agencies of the federal government that either make up their own laws or try to create their own law when they do not have law-making authority. … In this case, it appears that the Department of Defense under Obama—and probably at Obama's instruction—has decided

to ignore federal law and instruct the military to do things which are in fact illegal to do. ... And that is a very dangerous precedent for our Department of Defense—to do things that the law says that they're not allowed to do."

The article continues, "In May, the House of Representatives passed an amendment to the National Defense Authorization Act, authored by Akin, to make it clear that the 1993 federal Defense of Marriage Act (DOMA) applies to federal employees and federal property. DOMA not only protects states from being forced to accept homosexual marriages, it defines for federal purposes that marriage is between one man and one woman, said Akin."

Subsequent to this directive by Congressman Akins, President Obama announced that his administration could no longer defend the Defense of Marriage Act. SURPRISE! SURPRISE!

> **Homosexual military service support a sham**

(OneNewsNow.com, June 29, 2011)—To help get his program of unrestricted homosexual enlistment in the Armed Forces, a so-called poll was taken that indicated that seventy percent of military personnel were in favor of such an action. Elaine Donnelly, president of the Center for Military Readiness, did her own poll, and she reports that Obama's military poll was a sham, which we reported when it was taken. The seventy percent in favor was actually more like seventeen percent. Would our president actually lie to get homosexuals into our Armed Services?

> **Fighting back against sodomized military**

(OneNewsNow.com, December 29, 2010)—A report on military officers who were sickened by President Obama's edict ending 235 years of wholesome tradition of keeping homosexuals out of the U.S. Armed Forces. The opposition was led by spokesman Lt. Col. Bob Maginnis (ret.), who said, "You have a very corrupt regime running the country."

Perhaps so, but what we really have as commander-in-chief of the Armed Forces, according to some reports, is a former homosexual, or at least a bisexual, who never spent one day in any branch of the military. Inasmuch as the president is also the boss of our Armed Forces, in my opinion, no one should be allowed to run for the office of president without having served in some branch of the military.

> **U.S. military could be shut down by secret "back door" ...**
(WorldNetDaily.com, July 12, 2011)—The U.S. Navy purchased 59,000 microchips from China to be used in missiles and other equipment critical to combat procedures. However, it was discovered that these chips could be controlled from China. Was this purchase made with the approval and consent of the commander-in-chief? If not, why not?

> **Special Forces Wary of "Don't Ask" Repeal**
(NewsMax.com, December 28, 2010)—Military special forces departments, including Green Berets and Navy SEALS, were concerned that the unqualified enlistment of homosexuals would weaken our Armed Forces in general.

> **The unfriendly political environment**
(OneNewsNow.com, December 13, 2012)—Two lesbian marriage ceremonies were conducted at West Point in December 2012, evidently with Army chaplains presiding. Also, due to President Obama, commander-in-chief of all Armed Forces,

wanting all Army chaplains to perform same-sex marriages in the military services, Senator Jim Wicker (R-MS) and Senator Jim Inhofe (R-OK) have introduced a bill in Congress to protect chaplains from having to perform same-sex marriages. When President Obama signed the 2013 military budget bill providing some $633 billion or more for military expenses in 2013, he remarked that he signed it with reservations because part of the bill gave chaplains the option, as a matter of conscience, not to perform same-sex marriages.

➤ **Navy Sued Over Manipulation of "Gay" Data**
(WorldNetDaily.com, February 22, 2012)—In a lawsuit filed against the Navy, evidence was presented that President Obama, as previously referenced, did not tell the truth in presenting to Congress statistics that showed seventy percent of military personnel approved of homosexuals being in the Armed Forces, when the percentage of those who favored it was actually only seventeen percent.

➤ **Don't Ask, Don't Tell—Origin**
(Wikipedia.com)—The Uniform Code of Military Justice, signed by President Truman in 1950, clearly designated the policies and directives for discharging homosexuals from Armed Forces. The National Defense Authorization Act for fiscal year 1994, but passed by Congress in 1993, demanded that Armed Forces commanders abide by former law, rules, and traditions of not taking homosexuals in military units of national defense. Yet, on December 21, 1993, Bill Clinton, another president whose military service was limited or nonexistent, and whose morals were exposed when he was impeached, issued Defense Directive 1304.26, bypassing

Congress and the will of the people, which allowed homosexuals to join the Army, Navy, Air Force, or Marines under the guise of "Don't Ask, Don't Tell."

> **"I was in the middle of the viper's pit": Soldier describes gang rape as male-on-male sexual assault in the military increases**
>
> (*UK Daily Mail,* April 4, 2011)—Greg Jeloudov is an actor who had starring roles in movies such as *Braveheart* and *King Arthur.* Out of patriotism, he joined the Army in 2009, and was assigned to Fort Benning, Georgia. He reported that two weeks after arriving at the Army base, he was gang-raped by a number of soldiers, evidently homosexuals, in the showers. He said he was told the reason was that they wanted him to know who was in charge of the Army now. The article referenced a 2010 Pentagon report that affirmed the reason more soldiers do not report such sexual attacks is that "they don't want anyone else to know, don't think anything would be done about it, or are afraid of retaliation." Mr. Jeloudov said he thought about committing suicide after the attack.

> **Army approves atheism-themed concert at Fort Bragg**
>
> (Associated Press, August 8, 2011)—The U.S. Army approved for the soldiers at Fort Bragg a "Rock Beyond Belief" concert, in which, evidently, the Name of God will be mocked. Fort Bragg is one of the Army's largest bases, with 58,000 soldiers and 13,000 civilian workers. Those who attended heard the bad news from musicians and speakers their belief that there is no God.

> **U.S. Air Force Removal of "God" from Logo Sees Backlash**
>
> (*The Christian Post,* February 9, 2012)—The U.S. Air Force

caved in to pressure and removed the name of God from its logo "Doing God's Work" to "Doing Miracles." U.S. Representative Randy Forbes noted: "The Air Force is taking the tone that you can't use the Name of God, regardless of context in the military." This is what the Christian cleansing of America is all about. Also, subsequent to this act by the Air Force, a class in which Bible references were used to help pilots understand the moral position in what they need to do was discontinued.

> **Over 20,000 Sign Petition Over Banned Bibles at Military Hospital**

(*The Christian Post,* December 6, 2011)—Walter Reed Hospital is one of the largest, if not *the* largest, military hospital serving soldiers wounded in combat. Medical attention is also provided there for any soldier or veterans. The hospital recently issued an order stating that family (or anyone else) could take no religious items, including crosses, Bibles, or Christian literature to soldiers in the hospital. Who would be responsible for issuing such an order? President Obama is commander-in-chief of all Armed Forces and related affiliations. Why not ask him? The Navy said it would try to get the order rescinded, but whether that has been done or not is uncertain.

> **Strategic Importance of American Millennialism**

(Mjr. B. L. Stuckert, School of Advanced Military Studies, 2008)—This is a 72-page dissertation (which includes about twenty pages of references and "documentation") about the most dangerous element of the U.S. population that threatens our nation—*those who believe in a literal second coming of Christ, a Rapture to be followed by seven years of tribulation, and then a Kingdom of one thousand years ruled by Jesus Christ.* While several groups like the Jehovah's Witnesses and the Mormons are included, the main danger, the most dangerous enemies are pre-millennial believers. Who the author really is, or why this infamous diatribe was written is not known, at least by me. It seems though more than coincidental that it was released in 2008 when Barack Obama was running for president.

> **Navy's new gender-neutral carriers won't have urinals**
> (CNN.com, July 11, 2012)—It seems the Navy wanted to remind female sailors that they are women and have some major differences from men by installing urinals. Now, everyone will be treated equally—all will use the same bathrooms, or toilets, as the case may be.

In no other sphere of national life, communication, or law, has any president before President Obama dared to defy God. President Obama has placed this nation under the judgment of God. The Christian cleansing of America is nowhere more evident than in the military divisions—Army, Navy, Air Force, and Marines. Where are the pastors to challenge this abomination? There are a very few, but not many. This is why every Christian needs to pray for God to save this nation from those that would destroy it.

Chapter 4

The Role of Homosexuality in the Christian Cleansing in America

We have made several references to the unreasonable acceptance of homosexuality as a viable sexual alternative by the federal government, business entities, and certain Christian organizations and churches. We had rather skip this untenable subject, but, as a matter of conscience, we cannot.

AIDS as a terminal disease was first discovered in the late seventies or early eighties. It was then an unknown disease, and if it ever occurred in any individual before that time, there seems to be no record of it. It was discovered first, as far as is known, in homosexual males. It was, therefore, called GRID (gay-related immune deficiency).

In 1988, I had a heart bypass operation, and I refused to allow the hospital to use blood from the state blood bank, because at that time the procedure for detecting the virus in donated blood had not been perfected. I did not want to get AIDS from contaminated blood.

Where did AIDS come from? And why? The only answer I can give is that it is a curse upon this present generation. Jesus said that pestilences, international disease epidemics, would be a sign of the last days.

The culturally amoral condition of the Roman Empire at the time of the first coming of Jesus Christ seems to have been similar to that of the United States today. As Paul explains in the first chapter of his epistle to the Christians at Rome, homosexuality was a common practice in both the male and female population. The apostle wrote that even the women "burned in their lust one toward another." The only ones in Rome who seemed to be offended by this abomination were the Christians, on whom Emperor Nero poured tar and set them afire at night to light the avenues of Rome. So we see that Christian cleansing because of homosexuality was common two thousand years ago. Anyone who takes the correct biblical position against this terrible sin is immediately labeled homophobic.

As claimed in a book by Lawrence Sinclair, which seems to be authentic, the author claims he had a homosexual relationship with President Obama. In his first official speech after becoming president, Mr. Obama said that gays were the best people in the nation for public service and that he would appoint them to positions in the government, which he did. All of his czars, or presidential assistants, seem to be homosexuals, or at least most of them. The president said the federal government could no longer support DOMA, meaning marriage between one male and one female. Now, state after state seems to be recognizing marriage as also being between two men, two women, or whatever. This has been because of the support of the president to a sin that the Bible says will destroy any nation.

The worst epidemic that ever hit the United States was in 1918 when 500,000 died as a result of Spanish influenza. According to InfoPlease.com, as reported in the *World Almanac* and the by the U.S. Health Department, by 2005 in the U.S. 550,394 had died because of AIDS. However, on that same date, over 988,000 had contracted AIDS. Since 2005, those reported with AIDS probably have already died, making AIDS the deadliest plague ever to be imposed on the human race.

The World Health Organization in 2013 reported that in nations in equatorial Africa, fifty-nine percent of the women have HIV or AIDS. In 2012, my ministry, Southwest Radio Church, worked with several organizations to provide food and shelter for millions of African children, some with AIDS and some orphaned because their parents had died from AIDS. Yet, it is difficult now to get accurate statistics about AIDS because it is a politically protected disease, probably because of its association with homosexuals in government. This last year, President Obama signed a bill to permit immigrants with AIDS to migrate to the United States. Why? According to Newt Gingrich, in his book *Real Change,* AIDS victims in just three counties in Florida hit Medicare for over $400 million dollars in just six months. Now seniors are being shorted on Medicare because Medicare is going broke.

How many worldwide have died of AIDS? 30 million? 50 million? 100 million? Efforts by responsible Americans to report to the public this immense danger are rebuffed by both our government and the news media, and certainly it is a major factor in the Christian cleansing of America.

According to 2013 reports by the **World Health Organization**:
> **40 million people infected with HIV**
>> » 37.2 million adults
>> » 2.7 million children
> **28.1 million cases in Africa … mostly sub-Saharan**
> **2.3 million Africans die a year**
> **India is experiencing a meteoric rise in AIDS cases**
> **Russia and China expect an exponential epidemic**

Recent headlines include:

> **Obama Endorses Gay Marriage in Washington State, Maryland, Maine**
> (*Christian Post,* October 26, 2012)—Why would a president of the United States acclaim an anti-God, anti-Christian relationship between men and men?
> **Spriggs: Jump in lesbianism disproves "gay gene" theory**
> (OneNewsNow.com, November 17, 2011)—The claim by many that they are homosexuals because they were born that way is disproved by the fact that many in the government and society suddenly become homosexuals.
> **DC Council Considering Gay Divorce Bill**
> (Associated Press, January 10, 2012)—So-called gay marriage relationships are more unstable and violent than the traditional married couple. My Oklahoma City Gideon Club met weekly on Saturday mornings at a local chain restaurant on North May. One Saturday about twenty-five homosexuals

came in from a party, got in a fight, and broke dishes over each other's heads. Rather than try to clean the restaurant of AIDS-contaminated blood, the owners burned it down.

> **Middle School Apologizes for Gay Youth Organization's Inappropriate Talk**
> (*Christian Post*, November 6, 2012)—Public schools, evidently with the approval of the U.S. Department of Education, are observing "Diversity Day" to promote gay relations among students. One middle school in Maine apologized to parents for letting gays use it as a forum to promote homosexuality.

> **Hormonal treatments compliments of Calif. Taxpayers**
> (OneNewsNow.com, April 18, 2012)—California taxpayers must provide separate jails for transgenders and gays, along with hormone treatments.

> **Germany to ban sex with animals**
> (*London Daily Telegraph*, November 26, 2012)—Due to the rise and promotion of same-sex activity, all variant forms of this abomination are spreading. Some even want to marry their animals.

> **NIH under fire for grants toward creation of homoerotic website**
> (FoxNews.com, April 19, 2012)—The National Institute of Health has spent millions on websites to try to educate homosexuals of the dangers of getting HIV or AIDS.

> **Feds to hospitals: Go gay … or go broke**
> (OneNewsNow.com, November 19, 2010)—The U.S. Department of Health and Human Services has told all hospitals they must inform homosexual patients of their "special visitation" rights to designate "spouses," "domestic partners," family,

or friends in their visitation list, or any government-related insurance will not be paid to the hospital.

> **Pat Robertson Criticized for Suggesting Homosexuals Can Change**
> (*Christian Post*, December 21, 2011)—Homosexuals can change, but seldom do.

> **J.C. Penney stock crashes with news of gay marriage support**
> (American Family Association, July 17, 2012)—Businesses that hope to gain an increase in trade by supporting gay marriage usually experience the reverse. This is one way Christians can protest without being labeled homophobic.

> **HIV and AIDS by Sex and Race**
> (avert.org, August 19, 2010)—By sex, in the United States, three times as many males are infected with HIV and AIDS than females. By race, approximately twice as many black Americans have HIV or AIDS than white Americans, even though there are four times as many white Americans as black Americans.

> **Poll: Attitudes toward gays changing fast**
> (*USA Today*, December 5, 2012)—According to this report, nine out of ten Americans have changed their minds about homosexual activity to a more understanding and flexible one.

> **California Lawmaker Suggests Schools Teach Accomplishments of Gay Americans**
> (Fox40.com, December 13, 2010)—Enough said!

We have hundreds of similar news headlines to the ones above, but there is only so much that can be presented by an obvious spread of homosexuality in governments and general populations in this volume. *Ussher's Chronology* reports that in 1887 B.C. there was a huge explosion on the Syrian-African Rift, forty miles long, ten miles wide, and sixteen hundred feet deep. The cities of Sodom and Gomorrah, and their citizens, were killed instantly. This area today is known as the Dead Sea, where nothing grows. This place is given as a warning to all people that would give themselves over to the sin of homosexuality. But Jesus said that as it was in the days of Lot of Sodom, so it would be when He came again. If there is anything positive in all this, it is that when Jesus does come this sin will be obliterated off the face of the earth. In the New Heaven and the New Earth, there will be no homosexuals, no HIV or AIDS. The hope of a sin-sick world today is within the last prayer in the Bible: "Even so, come Lord Jesus" (Revelation 22:20).

Chapter 5

Christian Cleansing in the Family

The family is the basic unit of civilization. The family is the basic foundation of a local church, a community, or a nation. The family is like the brick in a building. If your roof leaks, you can get a carpenter. If your plumbing is bad, you can get a plumber; if your electric wiring is bad, you can get an electrician. But, if your bricks crumble, there is little, if anything, you can do to repair it. Of all the Christian cleansing progressing in the government, courts, Armed Forces, or anywhere else, the most dangerous and insidious is the Christian cleansing within the family unit.

The word "family" can apply to plants of a common variety, animals, birds, or even microbes. When applied to human beings, my *Webster's Dictionary* gives fifteen or more meanings of family, but the most common is, a group of people living in the same household of common ancestry. It can also be applied to the descendants of the common household and their descendants. Jesus is said to be of the family of David, proven in Matthew and Luke.

The Christian definition of a family is one man and one woman united by ceremony, love, and dedication for each other, so recognized by the church and state, including children that may be born within the marriage. Destroy the family and law enforcement problems increase, grocery stores go out of business, as well as many other kinds of businesses selling automobiles, clothing, etc. I once visited a kibbutz in Israel where there were no married couples, and everyone slept in a different bed every night. The Book of Jasper indicates this is somewhat the way it was at Sodom.

The following news stories concerning the weakening of the family unit are presented for serious consideration in saving the family unit of America:

> **Four in Ten Say Marriage Is Becoming Obsolete**
> (Associated Press, November 20, 2010)—Because almost half of the child population today is living with one parent or with grandparents, forty percent of Americans now, according to Pew Forum, believe it is useless for men and women to marry to produce children that become a burden to the rest. Forty-four percent of the U.S. population say they have or are now living with someone other than a legal husband or wife.

> **Voters approve same-sex marriage for the first time**
> (CNN.com, November 7, 2012)—Due to the promotion of homosexuality by the Obama administration, men are living with men and women with women in a so-called marriage arrangement that insults the meaning of marriage. A hundred men or women can rent property and live together legally, but such arrangements do not produce children or help sustain schools or other necessary organizations.

> **What June brings to Disney World**
> (OneNewsNow.com, April 20, 2012)—Disney World, a large entertainment park in Orlando, Florida, mainly for children and teenagers, dedicated all entertainment to homosexual, lesbian, transgendered, and cross-dressing lifestyles for 2012. The good news is that attendance was down by fifty percent.

> **CDC: U.S. Birth Rate Hits All-Time Low; 40.7% of Babies Born to Unmarried Women**
> (CNSNews.com, October 31, 2012)—The Aid for Dependent Children subsidy, which passed during the Johnson administration in 1966, encouraged some women to have more babies to get more money. In the last sixteen years, 80 million babies have been born in the United States with half, or 40 million, born out of wedlock (*World Almanac*). A high percentage of such children will usually have a criminal history and be a burden to society. There is no place like home.

> **Judge to mom: "You don't spank children"**
> (OneNewsNow.com, June 28, 2011)—If parents now follow the biblical rule of "spare the rod, spoil the child," they may end up in jail or have their children taken away from them. This is another indication of family authority being taken away from parents in the important mission of training a child in the way he or she should go.

> **Texas Mom Gets Probation, Loses Kids, for Spanking Her Daughter**
> (FoxNews.com, June 21, 2011)—This is a second article about the same Texas mom. A Corpus Christi mother was arrested, her daughter taken away from her, and she was given five years probation for, as the judge said, the crime of spanking

her daughter. The spanking was with an open hand, but the judge said that parents could not spank their children anymore. Parents have less authority, and the government more, for raising children.

> **Gay Marriage Gets First Ballot Win**
> (*Wall Street Journal,* November 7, 2012)—The article reports that fifty-two percent of Americans now approve gay marriage (so-called). This makes us wonder if over one-half of the nation's citizens have lost its sense of moral conduct. This further results in the demise of the family unit.

> **What parents don't know …**
> (OneNewsNow.com, February 15, 2012)—Seventy-four hundred girls from nine to thirteen years of age were given hormonal implants without parental consent in Great Britain. What happens in England usually also happens in the United States. This indicates the state has no respect for the family or parental authority over their children.

> **Preschooler's Homemade Lunch Replaced with Cafeteria "Nuggets"**
> (*Carolina Journal Online,* February 14, 2012)—One of many reports of schoolteachers or cooks replacing children's homemade lunch with cafeteria food. While this may be well intentioned, it not only decreases children's faith in their mothers, but it may not be as healthy as the original lunch.

> **FEMA's use of term "federal family" for government expands under Obama**
> (*Palm Beach Post,* September 1, 2011)—This article reports that FEMA and other federal agencies now refer to their operation as the "federal family." This is socialist or communist

terminology to get people, especially the younger generation, to look to the government rather than their family for help.

> **Suicide spikes among middle-aged women**
> (Today.com, July 27, 2011)—There is an alarming increase in suicides within the 40–69 age group. The breakup of the family unit, loss of communion with children, and possibly losing their husband to a younger woman, seem to be the causes.

> **Nearly Half of Americans Have Less Than $500 in Savings**
> (*Huffington Post*, October 23, 2012)—Considering that $2,000 a month is a bare minimum for the support of a family of four, this means that the average American family today has money to supply food and shelter for the family for only one week. This weakens greatly the stability of the average American family in many ways.

> **Salvation Army Seeing Record Number of Families in Need**
> (Minnesota—CBS News, December 7, 2012)—A record number of 18,000 families in Minneapolis registered for aid in one month, an example of the pressure the recession and the weakening of the dollar due to the increasing national debt is hurting the family financial structure.

> **Married couples at a record low**
> (*Washington Post*, December 13, 2011)—According to my concordance, there are 120 references to the family in the King James Version of the Bible. The institution of marriage and the family is the way that God chooses for men and women to live together and raise children in the fear and admonition of the Lord. As reported in the article, in 1960, seventy-two percent of adults were married, with the median age for brides being twenty and grooms being twenty-three. In 2012, only

fifty-one percent of the adults in America were married, with the median age for brides being twenty-seven and grooms being thirty. With the Obama administration championing the case for homosexual relationships, the number of marriage licenses in 2012 was exceedingly low.

> **Denver Drug Agent: Our Problems "Have Exploded" With Pot Legalization**
> (Denver—CBS News, December 13, 2012)—One of the most critical problems in the family is keeping children away from drugs. With many states now making pot and other types of mind-bending drugs legal, this will put more pressure on the family, with more children dying because of dope or ending up in jail.

> **Colorado to End Medicaid Coverage of Circumcision**
> (*Huffington Post,* June 23, 2011)—Most male babies at birth, especially those born in a hospital with a doctor's care, are circumcised. However, because circumcision in some cases is associated with a religious practice of faith, this important medical procedure, to some, will no longer be covered by insurance. This restriction has also spread to California and other states.

> **Top Earners Set to Pay Most, Especially Married People**
> (*Bloomberg News,* January 17, 2013)—I majored at the university in accounting, business administration, and tax accounting. When I went to work for Southwest Radio Church in 1951, I continued to do tax accounting at night and on the weekends. Under former federal income tax procedures, the husband and wife in a family setting could file a joint return and get a reduction in the amount of tax they would pay to

the federal government. Not so now on the Obama federal tax system. Married couples will be penalized and pay more taxes than single individuals, which favors the homosexual members of the population. This is also incentive for young unmarried members of the population not to marry and assume family responsibilities as commanded in the Bible.

The overall education and welfare programs today are purposely directed at the younger generation not to look to God or the family for temporal blessings, but to look to the almighty federal government.

Chapter 6

Christian Cleansing Via Immigration

From a Christian position, foreign immigration can be good or not so good. When anyone questions the not-so-good points of over-immigration, they are accused of narrow-mindedness, racism, or being un-Christian.

I have traveled and communicated with many people of other nations. I have drunk fermented mares' milk (UGH!) with Mongolians. I have enjoyed many missions to China. My booklet in Chinese, *Happiness,* that I wrote in 1978, soon after the trial of the Gang of Four, is still being used as a main evangelistic outreach by the Underground Churches in China. I even slept in a camel driver's tent one night in southern Jordan, but I had to pick fleas off my body for several days afterward. Here at the ministry, in 1985 we hired fifteen Cambodian refugees from the Killing Fields. I even married one—Kim Ky. We have now been married for over twenty-five years and I have a whole passel of step-grandchildren that look like Cambodians. So no one can accuse me of having racial hang-ups.

Oklahoma City, where I live, is a well-balanced, industrious city with many churches, mostly Southern Baptist. It has been recommended as a city for relocation due to low taxes, the low cost of housing, business opportunities, and a pro-industry attitude. Oklahoma City is also a multinational city.

We have a large Korean population, mainly in the southern section, who are good citizens and have their own Korean Christian churches. After the Vietnam War, several thousand Vietnamese immigrated to Oklahoma City. Most of them settled off of Classen Avenue north of Twenty-third Street, which at the time was an older part of the city and somewhat run-down. They rebuilt the old houses and refurbished and repaired the entire area. It is now one of the more beautiful parts of the city. Some have converted to Christianity, but most still go to their own Buddhist temples. But they are industrious, law-abiding, and most are now good American citizens.

We also have a fairly large population from India. Many have converted to Christianity, and one of their churches is close to our office. Most of the immigrants from India work in hospitals.

We also have a large Hispanic population that settled between Northwest Eleventh and Northwest Thirteenth streets, also an older section of the city. They too have made their own section of the city a much-improved and very nice section of the community. Three or four years ago though, thousands of illegal Hispanic immigrants settled in Oklahoma City. They took over parks and the malls during the day to get out of the heat and the weather. As in California and Arizona, construction companies hired them because they would work for half the rate of the legal carpenters and utilities workers. The city passed a law that any business concern that hired an illegal immigrant would be fined $50,000. In one week, all the illegals were gone.

Now, what has all this to do with the Christian cleansing of America?

The United States was settled by Christian pilgrims from England and other nations in Europe. Our founding fathers were Christians. Our national laws and customs are Christian in nature and purpose. Our founding fathers said that our Constitution would be good and the law of the land only as long as the United States was a Christian nation. According to statistics in the *2011 World Almanac,* there are over 10 million illegal immigrants living in the United States, and twenty percent of American homes speak a language other than English. When my wife came to the United States from Cambodia, where her parents and seven brothers died in the Killing Fields, she studied U.S. history, learned English, and became an American citizen.

Recently, President Obama made a national announcement that we no longer consider ourselves a Christian nation. It is true that due to increased immigration and the falling away of many churches from fundamental biblical truth, it may be debated as to whether this is still a Christian nation or not. But as far as I know, the president has no documentation for his claim. This seemingly indicates the president does not want this nation to be a Christian nation.

His national heritage background is Kenyan. His father and stepfather were both Muslims. His tutors were Marxists. His former church pastor in Detroit said that Mr. and Mrs. Obama were not church people, but that they joined his church for political purposes.

President Obama stated in his autobiography that at the university he always migrated to Marxist professors. As stated in *The Amateur,* the president is anti-colonial, anti-capitalist, and in some ways anti-American. In his inauguration speech for his second term, two of his statements were most interesting. He welcomed more foreign immigrants to the United States, and he promised equal rights to homosexuals, but what he must have meant was special rights.

Homosexuals hold jobs; they own property; because they have no family, they are richer than most; they can vote; and they can rent or own a house where they can live and perform sexual acts of a degrading nature without ever being questioned. What more equal rights do they want? What the homosexuals have to worry about the most—and the president didn't mention—was going to an everlasting Hell unless they repent and accept Jesus Christ as their Saviour.

Many, like my neighbors Mark and Ellen, sold everything they had and moved to Ecuador. They think this nation is going to become communistic. Doctors are moving to Costa Rica and other places. More immigration at this time will only make our nation decline as a Christian nation much faster. There are many reports now from the nations of Europe that multi-racism and multi-nationalism just isn't working, and they are trying to get their immigrants, especially the Muslims, to go back home.

One of the problems with Muslim immigration is that the average Islamic family has eight children. The average for the American family is two. There are now over two thousand mosques in the United States, and the number of mosques has increased seventy-four percent since Obama became president.

Europeans are now aware that they made a big mistake in allowing Muslim immigration. Several European nations have passed laws against building more mosques.

Estimates suggest that half of the 10 million-plus illegal immigrants in the United States are Muslim. President Obama, in his second inauguration speech, gave them citizenship status when they don't even know who the first president of the United States was, or what the Constitution is. If we make these 10 million illegals citizens, a year later there will be 20 million illegal immigrants in line for citizenship. Muslims do not come to the United States to become Americans. They come to the United States to be Muslims. The problem in Europe is that Muslims do not assimilate as Buddhists, Hindus, and adherents to other religions do.

Just a few of the many headline stories telling of the dangers of immigration, and especially Muslim immigration, are as follows:

> **Sharia lessons for pupils aged six: BBC uncovers "weekend schools" that teach pupils how to hack off thieves' hands**
> (James Slack, November 22, 2010)—In Muslim schools in England, students as young as six years of age are being taught how to cut off hands, and that Jews are their enemies whom they must kill.

> **Tampa "at risk" of Islamic takeover**
> (OneNewsNow.com, April 16, 2012)—Several cities in the United States, as has happened in Europe, are subject to Muslim takeover as has happened in Dearborn, Michigan.

> **Border Patrol Agents Pulled Off-Task**
> (OneNewsNow.com, November 9, 2011)—This news item referenced the Associated Press story on the Department of

Human Services, evidently on orders from the president, not to question any immigrant that was not intelligence driven. This new rule for checking immigrants will allow thousands to immigrate from Mexico into Texas, Arizona, and California with little or no information, many of whom may be Muslims from the Middle East entering the United States by way of Mexico.

> **Lawsuit: "Honor killings" OK by Michigan Shariah**
> (WorldNetDaily.com, February 22, 2011)—According to this report, there have been several honor killings in Michigan which were excused under sharia law. Under sharia law, a husband can kill his wife or children for what he considers conduct insulting or defaming to the family. This could be spread to other cities.

> **Iranian demonstrators threaten Esther's tomb**
> (*Jerusalem Post,* December 13, 2010)—Muslims have no respect for churches or other Christian sites. They are in control of Israel's most holy site—the Temple Mount.

> **Burning the Koran Is Worse Than Burning the Bible**
> (FoxNews.com, April 4, 2011)—Christians believe that the Bible was written by men led and inspired by God. Muslims believe that the Koran was written by God.

> **Muslim Prayers in the Streets of NYC**
> (Stand Up America blog, August 25, 2010)—Anyone who has driven in New York City understands the trouble in getting through its congested streets. Yet at Muslim prayer time, thousands of Muslims get on the street with their rugs and tie up traffic. If Christians did this they would be arrested, yet allowance is made for Muslims disobeying our laws.

> **Muslim Cleric Rips Up Bible at US Embassy Protest—Says Next Time His Grandson Will [Urinate] On It**
> (Jim Hoft, September 18, 2012)—This was done in front of the American Embassy in Cairo while thousands cheered.

> **Egypt Court Sentences 8 to Death Over Prophet Film**
> (Associated Press, November 28, 2012)—An Egyptian court sentenced eight Coptic Christians—whom they claimed had a part in the production of a film on the life of Mohammed—to death.

> **Islam in the United States**
> (Wikipedia.com)—Mohammed's army pillaged the Middle East and much of the orthodox Byzantine Empire, killing Christians and burning churches. The record of Mohammed reports that in one day he ordered the beheading of over eight thousand people. The anti-Christian dogma and deeds of Islam in the Balkans and Europe are history. Had Charles Martel of France not stopped the Islamic advance, all of Europe today might be Islamic, as well as the rest of the world. On eschatology, Islam teaches that the Mahdi (their Christ) will come and bring Jesus with him to kill everyone in the world who is not a Muslim. Yet, the United States continues to allow millions of Muslims to immigrate to the United States. The latest figures on Muslim immigration we could find indicated that 96,000 Muslims were allowed into the nation from the Middle East in 2005.

> **U.S. Lax on Screening Muslim Chaplains**
> (NewsMax.com, July 11, 2011)—In the 1970s I received some dozen or more letters from David Berkowitz, *aka* the Son of Sam. Later, at his trial for killing a number of people, the dis-

trict attorney of Queens, New York, subpoenaed the letters. Perhaps because of my witness to him, David became a Christian. Recently I called the prison in New York and asked to speak with David. I was told that I would have to go through the chaplain, but the imam was there at the time. The huge prison had a Muslim for a chaplain. I finally did get in touch with David. He was conducting Christian services that day, which was a Sunday, in the prison. Thousands of inmates are now being converted to Islam due to Muslim chaplains and other Muslim workers in the prison system.

The immigration policy of the United States is permitting millions of foreign immigrants into the United States who are traditional enemies of the church and Christians everywhere, and who believe that one day all Christians in the world will be exterminated. In this, our immigration policies are part of the Christian cleansing of America.

A few related news stories that need no comment or analysis:

» "Mexico Now Seeking Save of Immigrants"—*San Antonio Express* (October 10, 2012)
» "Egyptians Calling of Shariah Law—Islamic Caliphate"—*Israel Today* (August 3, 2011)
» "Christian Arab Predicts World Islamic Takeover … Unless …"—*Israel National News* (March 19, 2007)
» "U.S. Mosques Up 74% Since 2000"—*USA Today* (January 23, 2013)
» "More Americans Anti-America, Pro-Jihad"—*One News Now* (November 28, 2012)

- » "Lots of Mosques in the U.S."—*Wikipedia.com*
- » "Egyptian Jihad Calls for Removal of Pyramids"—*Al Arabiya* (November 12, 2012)
- » "Christian Convert from Islam Beheaded in Somalia"— *Morning Star News* (November 17, 2012)

Chapter 7

Christian Cleansing in the Sports Arena

Basketball, football, boxing, or collegiate athletics are usually not thought of as a Christian subject. However, in the modern setting almost everything people say, do, or think in some way relates to the Christian cleansing in the United States.

The Bible, as far as I know, says little on the subject except a reference to Corinth, where one of the largest of the first century Christian churches was located. I have been to Corinth many times, and it is always interesting to walk down the historical racetrack where Grecian athletes competed, and then stop at the Bema Seat where the victors were rewarded, usually with nothing more than a wreath of olive leaves. The Apostle Paul compared the steadfastness of Corinthian Christians to the running of a race:

> Know ye not that they which run in a race run all, but one receiveth the prize? So run, that ye may obtain. And every man that striveth for the mastery is temperate in all things. Now they do it to obtain a corruptible crown; but we an incorrupt-

ible. I therefore so run, not as uncertainly; so fight I, not as one that beateth the air: But I keep under my body, and bring it into subjection: lest that by any means, when I have preached to others, I myself should be a castaway.

—1 Corinthians 9:24–27

From A.D. 65 we go to A.D. 2013. Instead of an olive leaf wreath, sports gambling now runs into the billions of dollars. If you Google "sports gambling" on the Internet, you will be directed to a site where you can place a bet on one of the professional or college teams during any sports season.

In the 2011–2012 professional football season, the regular referees went on strike and substitute referees were hired. At one game, the replacement referees made a questionable call on a touchdown play, resulting in the loss of $300 million on this one play for some; for others, it was a $300 million win. There was a national furor for the referees' strike to be settled, which it was. The sin of gambling, in most cases, controls the course of national sports. I call gambling a sin, because everyone placing a bet is hoping that he can take money from someone else that he didn't have to work for.

According to the Sports Executive Association report of January 10, 2013, over $8 billion is bet on the Superbowl game, which determines the winner at the end of each football season. It is difficult now to even suggest any correlation between modern sports and the Christian race.

When I was in college back in the 1930s, it was quite common to have a prayer from a local pastor before the game began. Not so now. Now, in most major sports events, a rather heavy soprano will burst into a screeching high-C rendition of the "Star-Spangled Banner," our national anthem. By the time she reaches, "the land of the free and the home of the brave," she appears to be on the edge of exploding, or suffering in the final throes of birth pangs.

There is nothing wrong with the "Star-Spangled Banner," but I think it would have been good for Francis Scott Key to include something about God or the blessing of the Lord on our nation. I certainly would like to hear, occasionally at least, the national song made popular by Kate Smith in 1938—"God Bless America." But it is not going to happen. According to an article in *U.S. News & World Report* titled "About Sports Betting," betting on sports is illegal except in three or four states on a limited basis. In other words, those who bet on sports events, in most cases, are breaking the law. They are simply criminals who have not been caught. Millions of Christians are also involved. This same article reports that annually in the United States, illegal betting involves $390 billion, not counting the side bets of individuals.

Now you think that *U.S. News & World Report* would conclude that stricter laws are needed to stop the elderly, seniors on pensions, and widows from gambling away their money needed to preserve life. But no! The magazine uses the betting information to recommend that Congress **must legalize betting!**

If there are any dedicated Christians involved in sports, especially national sports, they almost always keep their relationship with the Lord—if they have one—a secret.

A few years ago, the Oklahoma University football team played the team from the University of Florida. On the Florida team, playing quarterback, was a young man with "John 3:16" printed in bold letters below his eyes. As I remember, the Florida team won. The young quarterback, named Tim Tebow, went on to win the Heisman trophy in 2007, and was the twenty-fifth pick in the 2010 annual professional football draft. He ended up as quarterback for the Denver Broncos. But what happened to Tim Tebow, a vocal Christian, in the professional sports circle?

> **Evangelical Football Star Tim Tebow Targeted for His Faith?**
> (ChristianPost.com, August 17, 2011)—Watching professional sports is not a regular habit of mine, but I do occasionally watch if local interests are involved, or if I might know of someone on the team. Tim Tebow started as quarterback for the Denver Broncos, and as usual there was "John 3:16" in plain white on black labels under his eyes. In the first half, the Denver team was behind. At halftime I looked, and there was Tebow on his knees in prayer, as he often did in college games. I thought perhaps I would go to bed, but then decided to watch and see if Tebow would be in the game after the half. He was, and he threw passes for 316 yards to match the 3:16 on his face. Denver won the game.

In later interviews with the press, Tebow credited his Christian faith with keeping him on course, living a clean life, and being rewarded by the Lord. Tebow was then accused of blasphemy, of being a religious nut, and a fantasy screwball. Regardless of his talents as a football quarterback, the consensus was that the Denver team could not handle the distraction of a religious player. Tebow was traded to the New York Jets, where his position is a second-string quarterback. He probably will not get to play football again. His career is over because of his faith.

> **Why They Can't Tolerate Tebow**

(*New York Post,* May 1, 2012)—This article is about an offer of $1 million to any girl who would swear that she had had sex with Tebow. The offer was legitimate because the football fans want to prove that Tebow is a fake. So far no girl has come to claim the $1 million, at least at the time of the writing of this book. The author of the article, Carol Markowicz, concluded: "It might not be for everyone, but Tim Tebow's refreshing, unpretentious, uncool personality seems to be the real, true him."

> **NASCAR Driver Loses Sponsor Over Christian Faith**

(ChristianNews.com, April 19, 2012)—Tim Tebow is just one example of Christian cleansing in the sports arena. NAS-CAR driver Blake Koch is another. The article referenced here reports: "Although many applaud the prayer meetings in NASCAR circles, not everyone is willing to tolerate Christian values on the racetrack. Indeed, NASCAR driver Blake Koch is being persecuted for his faith. Following California's Royal Purple 300, Koch sat just 28 points out of the top 10 driver standings—but he was forced to race with a blank car after losing his primary sponsor because of a controversy over his Christianity. Koch had partnered with The Rise Up and Register Campaign, which works to educate people on the importance of voting in the 2012 elections. But ESPN, would not allow the ad to air because of its so-called political and religious overtones. 'I didn't think that my faith in Christ would have an impact on whether or not a sponsor could air a commercial or not,' Koch told 'Fox and Friends' on March 29. 'The one thing I will not do is deny my faith just because a particular sponsor might not like the way I express my faith, which I do on my own time.'"

As the proverb goes, it's not who wins the race, but how the race is run. What place is there in the national sports scene for Christian athletes? Probably not much, if any. On football fields, baseball diamonds, basketball courts, and golf courses, Satan is busy washing them clean of Christians and God's Word. We live in perilous times. But keep the faith ... Jesus is coming soon!

In the Roman theaters of the first century A.D., thousands would come to see gladiators fight to the death. Also, on a huge sunken platform helpless victims would be imprisoned to await the charge of lions and tigers, to the screaming delight of the thousands of spectators. The huge mountainside theater at Ephesus which seated some 25,000 is still in good condition and opera groups from Europe frequently perform there even today. Engravings on one of the huge iron doors leading into the sunken stage depict lions and tigers. It was in this theater where Christians had to face these vicious and half-starved carnivorous animals. Paul said that he was among one group of Christians who had to fight the beasts of Ephesus (1 Corinthians 15:32).

But if we advance the calendar from A.D. 60 to A.D. 2013 we see on the TV twenty-four large men out on a playing field trying to run over each other, and the 50,000 attendant watchers screaming and yelling as stretchers rush out to carry away the wounded.

In many respects things have not changed. Sports has become largely an anti-Christian entertainment medium to keep Christians out of church and waste the Lord's money on gambling.

Chapter 8

Christian Cleansing in Science

A study on the subject of Christian cleansing in America would not be complete without referencing perhaps the most important item or medium that has been responsible for denying a special Creator and our relationship to Him—contemporary science.

Perhaps the most important evidence presented in the Bible relating to the very last days is found in Daniel 12:4, "… many shall run to and fro, and knowledge shall be increased."

I was born on December 11, 1922. The greatest thrill of my early years, as I remember, was getting up at four in the morning and riding with my father on a wagon full of cotton to the gin at the county seat, Hugo, Oklahoma. Perhaps once a day we would see an old Model T Ford come by the house. Occasionally we might see a two-wing single engine airplane that would be flying from Dallas to Oklahoma City.

Without the increase of knowledge as prophesied by Daniel for the last days, there would be no radios, no telephones, no automobiles, no airplanes, no computers, no air conditioning, or hundreds of electrical appliances that are important to the pursuit of happiness in our time. But I have in my ninety years seen all of these modern inventions become a reality. And neither would there be space travel or the atomic bomb. But Paul warned young Titus to "… beware of science, falsely so called." If this was true two thousand years ago, think how much more we should take Paul's advice today.

The one problem that scientists have not been able to prove or answer in a test tube is, Who are we? How did we get here? Where did we come from? and, Why are we here? The most advanced men of science in the first century A.D. were puzzled by these questions. Not being able to accept the truth that a mighty Creator who made the stars in the heavens and all things that do appear, even men, they proposed man came from the lower animal beings, much like the contemporary theory of modern science—evolution.

> Professing themselves to be wise, they became fools, And changed the glory of the uncorruptible God into an image made like to corruptible man, and to birds, and fourfooted beasts, and creeping things. Wherefore God also gave them up to uncleanness through the lusts of their own hearts, to dishonour their own bodies between themselves: Who changed the truth of God into a lie, and worshipped and served the creature more than the Creator, who is blessed for ever. Amen. For this cause God gave them up unto vile affections: for even their women did change the natural use into that which is against nature.   —Romans 1:22–26

According to Paul, the teaching of evolution will result in homosexuality, which is so rampant today that states are making legal the marriage of two men or two women.

> And likewise also the men, leaving the natural use of the woman, burned in their lust one toward another; men with men working that which is unseemly, and receiving in themselves that recompence of their error which was meet. And even as they did not like to retain God in their knowledge, God gave them over to a reprobate mind, to do those things which are not convenient.   —Romans 1:27–28

There is nothing wrong with knowledge, including scientific knowledge, as long as the Creator God is acknowledged. Take God out of knowledge, and as Paul said, nothing is left concerning the existence of man except the false theory of evolution. A belief in evolution and a biblical Creator are irreconcilable. Trying to believe in both results in theistic evolution, which is myth void of truth.

At the time I was in the South Pacific with my Army unit during World War II, I was not a Christian. Waiting out the long days and nights in moving from one island to the next resulted in boredom. To pass the time, five or six of us would get into a twenty-five cent poker game. No one ever won or lost much, but it did help pass the time. We played by the rules. But what if, in a poker game, one person wanted to change the rules with every new deal? If he saw he had been dealt two deuces, the lowest pair would win. The next deal perhaps he would get two aces, and then he would want to change the rules so that the highest pair won. No one would want to play with someone like that.

However, in our schools today, from kindergarten to the university, we let the scientists and educators play by their rules. As Paul noted in Romans, this is what always happens. The scientist cannot accept the truth that there is a Creator who is smarter than he is. Although Charles Darwin is the so-called originator of the theory of evolution, he was not the first to have this idea. In order to come up with a believable answer as to what man is, where he came from, and why he is here, the old untried myth is revived with unconnected genetic "facts" woven into a theory that supports the unproven conclusion that mankind evolved from lower life forms over millions of years.

In the final analysis, the theory of evolution is not a scientific conclusion, but a false education proposition to try to prove there is no God. We let the scientists call the rules, and they get away with it.

What if scientists at NASA announced that space probes prove that Jupiter, the largest planet in our solar system, is made of green cheese? Reason would tell us that would be impossible. In all theories and postulates, reason rules. Does it seem reasonable that over millions of years lower life forms evolved into thousands of other forms of life in the animal, reptile, fowl, and marine species? Not only does the theory of evolution propose this fantasy, it also proposes that all forms of life referred to above evolved into male and female to produce offspring and add to DNA the advancements made from lower forms of life. Reason tells us that such a theory is impossible.

In the first place, from where did these supposed lower life forms come? Who made them, or how did they evolve? The course of higher contemporary education is to disprove the reality that only a Master Creator who is more powerful than we can imagine created everything in the universe.

In other areas of scientific lunacy, President Obama has come up with the scarecrow that we may all die from global warming. This idea originated in the United Nations in 1993 to unite all nations against a common foe or danger. What was concluded was that global warming due to an increase of CO_2 in the air was the cause, and that all nations should unite in getting rid of this danger. Billions of dollars have been wasted by the present administration to pursue this folly.

Dr. Edward Blick, a professor of science at the University of Oklahoma, and a weatherman for the Air Force and NASA, is also a trustee of Southwest Radio Church Ministries. We have published two books by Dr. Blick disproving this political scam. There is no global warming. In fact, the latest weather statistics indicate we have global cooling. As far as CO_2, the main supposed enemy, is concerned, animals breathe in oxygen and give off CO_2. Plants use CO_2 and give off oxygen. God made it that way. As much as ninety-seven percent of CO_2 comes from the oceans. If CO_2 is a danger, then all carbonated drinks should be taken off the market.

Another source of controversy is medical science. The kind of medical care a patient gets is often determined by his or her ability to pay. However, any person with an acute medical problem can go to the emergency ward of any hospital and receive medical attention. Recently, Brother Alex Mathai, a missionary from India, called me. He shared that he had a serious heart problem, but he had no money and no health insurance. He wanted to know if I could help him. I called my own heart doctor, also a dear friend, who goes on foreign missions with me all the time. Dr.

Sutor advised me to tell Brother Alex to check in at the emergency ward of the hospital where he was on duty that weekend. Brother Alex did, and Dr. Sutor did a heart procedure on him, removed the blockage, kept him overnight in the hospital, and sent him home the next morning. Brother Alex said he got a bill for $72,000 … but it was marked PAID!

Under the Obama healthcare bill, medical assistance has been promised to every individual in the country. Hundreds of employers have dismissed thousands or millions of employees because employers who had been paying, or helping pay, employees' insurance find the new insurance rates so high they can't afford them. Senator Tom Coburn (R-OK) shared on our program that eighty-three percent of the doctors have said they could not operate under the Obama healthcare arrangement. Many of them are leaving for Costa Rica or other countries. New hospitals are being built for these doctors. The wealthiest Americans can catch a plane and go to one of these hospitals, but the lower and middle wage earners cannot afford the high costs. If politics, greed, and the theory of evolution could be taken out of contemporary science, it would be a blessing instead of a curse.

How many young people of yesterday, today, and tomorrow will go to an everlasting Hell because they have been tricked into believing that they evolved from lower life forms rather than from a Creator who sent His only begotten Son so that they would have eternal life? The number is in the millions, or perhaps billions. While we owe to science much for the benefits of modern life, they are at the top of the list among those promoting Christian cleansing in the nation today. Yet, most pastors never attempt to explain to their congregations the danger of believing in the theory of evolution for fear of offending some in the audience.

The following headline news stories have unlimited prophetic relevance:

> **Spanish Researchers Want to Tag Human Embryos with Bar Codes**
> (FoxNews.com, December 13, 2010)—There have been limited efforts to microchip individuals, even school children, for identification and control purposes. Now government scientists want to barcode babies before they are born.

> **Government OKs Controversial Research Into Artificial Life Forms**
> (FoxNews.com, December 16, 2010)—A presidential commission has given the University of Pennsylvania permission to create new life forms.

> **Countdown to the Apocalypse: Scientists to Change Doomsday Clock**
> (FoxNews.com, January 17, 2007)—This article has a subhead: "The end of the world may be drawing a bit closer."

> **Invisibility cloak now a reality, scientists say**
> (FoxNews.com, November 13, 2012)—Scientists have finally solved the problem of being invisible. God said whatever man could imagine, that he could also do.

> **Underwater Cities, Ruins and Other Urban Archaeology: 7 Submerged Wonders of the World**
> (WebUrbanist.com, September 12, 2007)—Scientists evidently are not able to explain how seven large cities have been found on the ocean floor, unless the biblical account of the Flood of Noah's day is true.

➤ **Underwater Cities; Noah's Flood Proof? …**
(s8int.com, December 14, 2010)—We read in the Genesis account in the Bible that Cain went out and built a city. We assume that others before the Flood also built cities. This is an extensive article of several pages in length. It includes pictures of cities with large buildings and streets that are several hundred feet deep on the ocean floor.

➤ **Doomsday for Iran? US Tests EMP Bomb**
(ArutzSheva.com [Israel], December 5, 2012)—The latest in a series of nuclear bombs that could destroy a nation.

➤ **China military eyes preemptive nuclear attack in event of crisis**
(KyodoNews.com, January 5, 2011)—China warns they could start a nuclear war if they feel threatened.

➤ **New chip raises fears of the end of privacy**
(*Washington Times,* January 23, 2003)—This article from ten years ago reports on concerns that in the future, by law all Americans will be computer-chipped.

➤ **Group Fears RFID Chips Could Herald "Mark of the Beast"**
(AgapePress.com, March 29, 2005)—A warning that the Bible could be true concerning prophecies about the mark of the beast.

➤ **CDC Warns Untreatable Gonorrhea Is On the Way**
(*U.S. News & World Report,* February 13, 2012)—The Centers for Disease Control warns that drug-resistant sexually transmitted diseases are now in evidence.

➤ **Obamacare vs. religion**
(Associated Press, open date)—Forty Catholic entities have sued the Obama administration for trying to force them to

pay for abortions and contraceptives, which is against their beliefs and practices.

> **PICKET: Companies plan massive layoffs as Obamacare becomes reality**
> (*Washington Times,* November 8, 2012)—The current administration's healthcare bill is already putting many out of work. Others will have to drop their health insurance due to high costs.

> **EU to ban cars from cities by 2050**
> (*London Telegraph,* March 28, 2011)—Science has had its heyday, so its back to the horse and buggy for Europeans.

> **Obamacare just raised your health care premium by $63**
> (HotAir.com, December 11, 2012)—Under the Obama healthcare bill, health insurance will cost much more.

> **Dems Facing Sticker Shock for Obamacare**
> (WorldNetDaily.com, December 20, 2012)—The cost of insurance for one employee under Obamacare could be as much as $17,500 per year.

> **Surprise: PA College Slashes Instructors' Hours to Avoid Obamacare**
> (Breitbart.com, November 21, 2012)—Pennsylvania Community College cut the hours of over four hundred full-time and part-time employees to avoid the high insurance costs of Obamacare.

> **Both House and Senate Health Bills Require the Microchipping of Americans**
> (Food and Drug Administration, March 18, 2010)—H.R. 3200, pages 1001–1008, mentions as a requirement that implantations be made in the patient wherever needed. The bill does

not specifically mention a microchip, but it could be included.

> **New "superbug" may be killing hundreds**
> (*London Telegraph,* November 19, 2007)—New forms of disease appear as scientists find cures for present ones.

> **Blood moon eclipses: 2nd Coming in 2015?**
> (WorldNetDaily.com, April 30, 2008)—NASA's website predicts a series of solar and lunar eclipses and other signs on holy days in 2015. WorldNetDaily asks if these are the signs in the sun and the moon that will announce the second coming of Jesus Christ.

> **31,000 scientists reject "global warming" agenda**
> (WorldNetDaily.com, May 19, 2008)—Scientists in various fields of weather control, geology, and related sciences say there is no global warming.

> **HAARP Poses Global Threat**
> (*Pravda,* June 10, 2008)—Russian newspaper *Pravda* charges the U.S. HAARP project in Alaska is causing worldwide hurricanes, tornadoes, and earthquakes.

> **Boeing Plans to Fly Tourists to Space**
> (*New York Times,* September 15, 2010)—As early as 2015, Americans may be able to visit Mars, but must provide their own oxygen, water, and sandwiches.

> **Does "God Particle" Exist? Scientists to Decide by 2012 Year's End**
> (ChristianPost.com, July 26, 2011)—The European Organization for Nuclear Research believes there is a God particle that will explain everything about the universe, including the Christian belief in Heaven. So far in 2013, there is no further news.

➤ **Energy saving bulbs "release cancer causing chemicals," say scientists**

(*Daily Mail* [UK], April 20, 2011)—The older, cheap light bulbs have been outlawed, forcing Americans to buy the new ones at three or four times the price. Now it seems the so-called "safe" light bulbs may be more dangerous to your health than the old ones.

Chapter 9

Christian Cleansing in the Judiciary

Congress shall make no law respecting an establishment of religion, or prohibiting the free exercise thereof; or abridging the freedom of speech, or of the press; or the right of the people peaceably to assemble, and to petition the Government for a redress of grievances

—The First Amendment to the Constitution of the
United States, part of the Bill of Rights

Sometime in the 1770s before the writing of the Declaration of Independence, Stephen Girard left France and immigrated to the British colonies of America. He eventually settled in Philadelphia, Pennsylvania, where he died in 1831.

Girard's wife had already passed away, and they had no children. Being exceptionally wealthy, Girard wanted some of his estate to go toward the establishment of a school for male orphans in Philadelphia. His brother and some of his nieces contested the will, and the case made it all the way to the Supreme Court.

One of the issues before the Court was the stipulation in Girard's will that although the boys were to be taught morals as part of their education, no ministers of any religious or Christian denomination were to be allowed on the school grounds. Girard stated that he had no animus toward Christianity; he just felt that there were so many different Christian sects and denominations in the United States, all with differing beliefs, that no preference should be shown toward any one denomination or church. According to the online edition of Legal Dictionary, Girard's relatives stated that they believed this stipulation violated not only the Constitution of the United States, but also

> ... the common law, and the public policy of Pennsylvania. The purported violations consisted of (1) excluding all religious personnel of any sect from positions within the college or from visiting the premises and (2) limiting instruction to purely moral concepts of goodness, truth, and honor, thereby implicitly excluding all instruction in the Christian religion.
>
> —Legal Dictionary, *Vidal v. Girard's Executors*

Justice Joseph Story wrote the unanimous 1844 decision for the Court. Again quoting Legal Dictionary online:

> The Court ruled that Girard had adopted a position of neutrality with respect to the exclusion of all religious influence from the administration of the college. He had not explicitly impugned Christianity, which, in a qualified sense, was a part of the common law of Pennsylvania, or any other religion. Rather, he had merely wanted the students to remain free from sectar-

ian controversy and wished them to study a curriculum that did not place inordinate emphasis on religious subjects. He did not proscribe members of the laity from teaching the general principles of Christianity or analyzing the Bible from a historical perspective. The Court concluded that Girard's provisions did not contravene the laws, the constitution, or the public policy of Pennsylvania.

This case is famous for Justice Story's defense of Christianity and his affirmation of the right of schools to teach the Bible and Christianity to students. He wrote:

> Why may not laymen instruct in the general principles of Christianity as well as ecclesiastics. There is no restriction as to the religious opinions of the instructors and officers. They may be, and doubtless, under the auspices of the city government there will always be men not only distinguished for learning and talent, but for piety and elevated virtue, and holy lives and characters. And we cannot overlook the blessings, which such men by their conduct, as well as their instructions, may—nay must—impart to their youthful pupils. Why may not the Bible, and especially the New Testament, without note or comment, be read and taught as a divine revelation in the college—its general precepts expounded, its evidences explained, and its glorious principles of morality inculcated? What is there to prevent a work, not sectarian, upon the general evidences of Christianity, from being read and taught in the college by lay teachers? Certainly there is nothing in the will that proscribes such studies.

Jay Sekulow, founder of the American Center for Law and Justice, and Jeremy Tedesco wrote in "The Story Behind *Vidal v. Girard's Executors*" that this case was extremely important concerning religious liberty in the United States. They believe that

> it demonstrates the view of the United States Supreme Court in the nineteenth century regarding an issue that has bedeviled the Court nearly its entire history: The proper role of religion in public schools. In *Vidal*, Joseph Story decided that religion played a vital role in public education, and upheld the use of the Bible and the teaching of Christian moral principles in a city-run school.

Fast forward to January 2013: Fox News reported that the Conway public school district in Arkansas banned religious leaders from school campuses because Wisconsin's Freedom From Religion Foundation filed a complaint against the school.

> The practice of allowing youth ministers to visit students during the lunch hour has been a longtime tradition in many Southern states. Murry, who became superintendent six years ago, said the practice had been in place long before he arrived. And until recently, not a single person had complained.
>
> —Fox News, Todd Starnes, "Public School
> Bans Religious Visitors," January 2013

In a letter to the school district, Patrick Elliott, an attorney with the Freedom From Religion Foundation wrote:

> It is inappropriate and unconstitutional for Conway Public

Schools to offer Christian ministers unique access to befriend and proselytize students during the school day on school property. No outside adults should be provided carte blanche access to minors—a captive audience—in a public school. This predatory conduct is inappropriate and should raise many red flags. … In many cases, we have found that the pastor uses the school to befriend students with the goal of spreading a Gospel message and recruiting members for his church's youth group. This sort of entanglement between religion and public education is unseemly and inappropriate.

The school district is now being represented by Liberty Institute, a law firm known for handling religious liberty cases. How did we come from being a nation whose courts rejoiced in teaching the Bible in schools to a country in which you can't mention God at a high school graduation ceremony without the threat of being thrown in jail? *Vidal v. Girard's Executors* is not the only court decision affirming the United States' Judeo-Christian heritage.

In 1811, New York's state supreme court affirmed a lower court ruling in the case of a man who was distributing pamphlets cursing and defaming God, Jesus Christ, and the Bible. The court's decision stated, "[W]hatever strikes at the root of Christianity tends manifestly to the dissolution of civil government."

The Supreme Court issued a unanimous decision in the case of *Church of the Holy Trinity v. U.S.* in 1892. "[N]o purpose of action against religion can be imputed to any legislation, state or national, because this is a religious people … this is a Christian nation."

This was the official position of American courts until 1947 and the Supreme Court's decision in *Everson v. Board of Education.*

Justice Hugo Black, a member of the Ku Klux Klan in Alabama, lifted an obscure phrase from a private letter Thomas Jefferson wrote to the Danbury Baptist Church in 1802, "wall of separation between Church and State." Justice Black deliberately perverted Jefferson's meaning in his letter to the church when Black wrote:

> No tax in any amount, large or small, can be levied to support any religious activities or institutions, whatever they may be called, or whatever form they may adopt to teach or practice religion. Neither a state nor the Federal Government can, openly or secretly, participate in the affairs of any religious organizations or groups and vice versa. In the words of Jefferson, the clause against establishment of religion by law was intended to erect "a wall of separation between Church and State."

The use of this phrase by Justice Black, which was without legal precedent in the United States, has been cited since 1947 to justify the removal of every vestige of our Judeo-Christian heritage from every aspect of American government, culture, and society. This includes banning prayer and the singing of Christmas carols in public schools; the removal of the Ten Commandments from schools and courthouses; and the removal of Christmas trees and Nativity scenes in public. The following are some recent examples of how groups are using that phrase to eliminate Christianity and the Bible in our country.

In November 2012, the *Los Angeles Times* reported that a federal judge ruled that the city of Santa Monica, California, could ban Nativity scenes, including one that had been on display for nearly sixty years. Supporters of the Nativity scenes were disappointed, while the attorney representing the city was "pleased."

Alsip, Illinois, didn't even wait for a lawsuit to be filed by the Freedom From Religion Foundation before they caved over a Christmas cross on the town's water tower. The threat of an expensive court case was enough for Alsip to abandon a tradition going back to the 1970s and replace the cross with a "holiday tree." The Freedom From Religion Foundation's co-president, Annie Gaylor, was thrilled. She said, "Towns can't put crosses on public structures such as water towers because we have separation between religion and government" (TheBlaze.com, November 20, 2012, "Water Tower Christmas Cross to Be Replaced With 'Holiday Tree' in IL Town").

In 2008, Elaine's Photography in Albuquerque, New Mexico, was approached by a woman who wanted the business to photograph a "commitment" ceremony with her lesbian partner. Because the owners, Elaine and Jon Huguenin, were Christians, they politely declined but "thanked her for her interest." The lesbians filed a lawsuit against Elaine and her husband on the grounds of discrimination. So far, every court has ruled in favor of the lesbians, fining the Christian business owners almost $7,000.

Elaine Huguenin has said, "If it becomes something where Christians are made to do these things by law in one state, or two, it's going to sweep across the whole United States ... and religious freedom could become extinct." Some think this case could go all the way to the Supreme Court.

A student at the Connellsville Junior High School in Connellsville, Pennsylvania, enlisted his parents and the Freedom From Religion Foundation to sue over a display of the Ten Commandments on school property in September 2012. TheBlaze.com reports, "According to the FFRF and its clients, the structure violates the First Amendment, so they are asking the court to order that it be removed from the school's property" (TheBlaze.com, September 28, 2012, "Atheists Sue Over 10 Commandments Display at PA Middle School"). The atheists are also demanding that the Ten Commandments plaque not even be allowed on the property of a nearby church because students can see it from the school!

Fox News reported on January 12, 2012, about the ruling of a judge who ordered that a prayer mural that had been hanging in a Rhode Island school since 1963 be removed simply because one student was offended.

> A federal judge has ruled that a Rhode Island high school must tear down a prayer banner that encouraged students to be kind and helpful because it offended non-Christians and was a violation of the U.S. Constitution. U.S. District Court Judge Ronald Lagueux ruled that the prayer banner at Cranston High School West must be removed immediately because it promotes religion. Jessica Ahlquist, an atheist student, had sued the city of Cranston and the high school after they initially refused to remove the banner. The prayer, which has been posted at the school for decades, begins with the words "Our Heavenly Father" and ends with "Amen." It encouraged students to be kind, to do their best in school and to learn the true value of friendship.

These are only a few of the hundreds of examples that could be given about what is currently happening to Christians and Christianity throughout the United States.

Consider the case of the Hernandez family in San Antonio. Steve Hernandez and his family are devout evangelical Christians. They have objected to their daughter, Andrea, wearing an RFID tracking chip that John Jay High School is forcing on all the students. The school says they are losing millions in federal funding because they are not able to obtain an accurate daily count of all the students that attend the school.

According to NBC News, the school district's communications director, Pasqual Gonzalez, justified the $261,000 chip tracking system. "The revenues that are generated by locating kids who are not in their chairs to answer 'present,' but are in the building—in the counselor's office, in the cafeteria, in the hallway, in the gym—if we can show they were, in fact, in school, then we can count them present."

Mr. Hernandez feels that the RFID chips are just one more step leading to the "mark of the beast" in the Book of Revelation. He told NBC News, "My daughter should not have to compromise [her] religion just because Northside Independent School District wants to get paid."

Although the ACLU has been at the forefront of suing schools to remove displays of the Ten Commandments and other religious artifacts from schools and government buildings, the group supports the Hernandez family and has described the tags as "dehumanizing." Jay Stanley with the ACLU office in Washington, D.C. said, "What kind of lesson does it teach our children if they're chipped like cattle and their every movement tracked? It doesn't create the kind of independent, autonomous people that we want in our democratic society."

The school retaliated against Andrea for refusing to wear the chip. She said she was not allowed to vote for homecoming king and queen. TheBlaze.com reported on October 8, 2012, what happened.

> "About two weeks ago when I went to cast my vote for home-coming king and queen I had a teacher tell me I would not be allowed to vote because I did not have the proper voter ID," Andrea said. "I had my old student ID card which they origi-nally told us would be good for the entire four years we were in school. He said I needed the new ID with the chip in order to vote."

In January 2013, a federal court ruled in favor of the school and ordered Andrea to either wear the chip her school required or transfer to another school without an RFID chip tracking system.

You may think that giving the Hernandez family the option of transferring Andrea to another school that doesn't use RFID chips solves the problem. And it does ... temporarily. But what happens when all public schools in the U.S. require RFID tags for their students? Americans currently have the right to homeschool their children or put them in private schools. What if these options are no longer available or unaffordable for many families?

You may think this could never happen in the United States. But how many things have happened in our country since 2001 that we thought we would never see? A country that has pub-lic schools mandating tracking chips for students will probably demand all children be enrolled in that system—whether they want to be or not.

Schools are not the only targets of those wanting to erase any semblance of Christianity in our nation. President Obama's administration is using the Affordable Health Care Act, more commonly known as Obamacare, to stop Christians from owning and operating private companies and businesses.

Christy Industries in St. Louis, Missouri, is a refractory distributor. Its owners, the O'Briens, are Catholics who do not believe they should be forced to provide health insurance to their employees that cover abortion, contraception pills, and sterilization surgeries, which the Obamacare law now demands. The O'Briens are only one of the plaintiffs in a lawsuit against the Obamacare mandates. Frank O'Brien, the CEO of Christy Industries, charges, "In essence, if you are Catholic in this country, you no longer can own a company. ... By means of this law, the Obama administration has mandated that no Catholic can own a business and provide health insurance to their employees without incurring crippling fines."

The *National Review* article (December 31, 2012, "Let's Be Frank") goes on to report that the Justice Department is taking the amazing position that a Christian cannot own or operate a business.

> This posture is one that the Department of Justice has been defending in court, arguing that an individual makes a choice to put these religious-liberty claims aside when he decides to run a company. "Once someone starts a 'secular' business, he categorically loses any right to run that business in accordance with his conscience," explains Kyle Duncan of the Becket Fund for Religious Liberty. "The business owner simply leaves her First Amendment rights at home when she goes to work at the business she built. Kosher butchers around the country must be

shocked to find that they now run 'secular' businesses. On this view of the world, even a seller of Bibles is 'secular.'"

Hobby Lobby is another business being targeted by the Obama administration. Hobby Lobby has stores in forty-one states but is owned by the Green family, evangelical Christians who refuse to comply with the pro-abortion, anti-family Obamacare mandates and are also suing the federal government. Unlike Christy Industries, a federal appeals court refused to give Hobby Lobby an exemption from the Obamacare mandates while the case is being considered by the courts. Hobby Lobby is being fined $1.3 million per day for violating the Obamacare law.

Most Americans have no idea that the founders took many of their ideas on law from William Blackstone, who based his *Commentaries on the Laws of England* on the Bible and the Ten Commandments. His *Commentaries* were required reading and studying for law students in college or anyone else wanting to practice law in the American colonies, among them John Adams and Patrick Henry. The following quotes are only a few from William Blackstone:

No enactment of man can be considered law unless it conforms to the law of God.

Blasphemy against the Almighty is denying His being or Providence or uttering *contumelious* [humiliating contempt or insult] reproaches on our Savior Christ. It is punished at common law by fine and imprisonment, for Christianity is part of the laws of the land.

To instance in the case of murder: this is expressly forbidden by the Divine. ... If any human law should allow or enjoin us to commit it, we are bound to transgress that human law.

Considering the Creator only as a being of infinite power, he was able unquestionably to have prescribed whatever laws he pleased to his creature, man, however unjust or severe. But, as he is also a being of infinite wisdom, he has laid down only such laws as were founded in those relations of justice that existed in the nature of things antecedent to any positive precept. These are the eternal immutable laws of good and evil, to which the Creator himself, in all his dispensations, conforms; and which he has enabled human reason to discover, so far as they are necessary for the conduct of human actions.

In general, all mankind will agree that government should be reposed in such persons in whom these qualities are most likely to be found the perfection of which is among the attributes of Him who is emphatically styled the Supreme Being; the three great requisites, I mean, of wisdom, of goodness, and of power: wisdom, to discern the real interest of the community; goodness, to endeavour always to pursue that real interest; and strength, or power, to carry this knowledge and intention into action. These are the natural foundations of sovereignty, and these are the requisites that ought to be found in every well-constituted frame of government.

It can be stated with confidence that few, if any, law students today are familiar with Blackstone or his positions on Christianity and the law.

In 2008, Michelle Obama gave a campaign speech in San Juan, Puerto Rico, in which she revealed the strategy we have seen the president, the first lady, and their allies implement during his first administration and which will continue for at least his second administration. She said, "Barack knows that we are going to have to make sacrifices; we are going to have to change our conversation; we're going to have to change our traditions, our history; we're going to have to move into a different place as a nation."

The president and the first lady are deliberately changing the history, the culture, and the traditions of the United States of America. Their goal is a godless, atheistic, amoral nation that is completely detached from this country's Judeo-Christian history, morals, traditions, and founding.

If President Obama and his administration are successful, eventually no American of any Judeo-Christian religious affiliation, including Protestants, Catholics, Baptists, evangelicals, and even orthodox Jews will be allowed to own or operate a business in the United States. How long will it be before these same Americans will be barred from working in a business or attending a public school?

> **Federal Judge Rules North Carolina's "Choose Life" License Plate Unconstitutional**
  (FoxNews.com, December 11, 2012)—According to Wikipedia, twenty-seven states allow "Choose Life" license plates for automobiles; another fifteen are considering allowing the license plates. But U.S. District Court Judge James Fox ruled in December 2012 that North Carolina's "Choose Life" license plates were unconstitutional. Why? Because "in his judg-

ment," the license plate violates the First Amendment, which is supposed to guarantee religious freedom in the U.S.! The judge continued that it was unfair for North Carolina to offer a pro-life license plate and not offer a pro-abortion license plate. This decision puts the rights of Americans to purchase "Choose Life" license plates in jeopardy in other states. This is just one more example of how convoluted our courts have become in flagrantly disregarding the rights of religious Americans in our country.

> **Santa Monica Can Ban Nativity Scenes, Judge Rules**
  (*Los Angeles Times,* November 19, 2012)—Local churches in the Santa Monica area had displayed Nativity scenes since the 1950s. In 2011, the city held a lottery for holiday displays when requests outnumbered venues. It is amazing (and, may I say, improbable) that atheists won eighteen of the available spots; churches won only two. Of course, the churches were upset so in 2012, the city decided to ban the private displays, and a judge agreed.

> **Southern California Christian School Goes to Court Over Religious Liberty**
  (DailyCaller.com, January 28, 2013)—In 2009, Calvary Chapel of Thousand Oaks, California, bought a school and turned it into a religious for-profit Christian school with a Christian curriculum. When church leaders in 2012 asked teachers at the school to submit verification of their religious faith from a pastor, two teachers refused, demanding $150,000 and threatening to sue. Calvary Chapel has filed a lawsuit to protect itself from extortion, saying they have the right to employ or fire anyone they want in accordance with their religious stan-

dards which are protected under the First Amendment. Rev. Rob McCoy, headmaster of the school said, "We wanted to make sure teachers subscribed to that faith. ... Any for-profit company that is owned by a religious organization will not have the religious freedom to exercise their beliefs." McCoy warned that the outcome in this case will affect churches of every denomination.

> **Supreme Court Rejects Christian Clubs' Appeal on School's Nondiscrimination Policy**

(ChristianPost.com, March 20, 2012)—Two Christian groups at San Diego State University—Alpha Delta Chi and Alpha Gamma Omega—wanted to elect leaders for their groups that agree with their Christian statements of faith. Because the university said that the Christian sorority and fraternity were in violation of religious and sexual orientation policies, the groups were not entitled to student funding, not allowed to post notices on campus, and not allowed to advertise on the university's website. This is tantamount to a blackout of these Christian groups, and they have struggled to survive on campus. David Cortman, an attorney for the Alliance Defense Fund who was representing the Christian groups, said that the university's position would be equal to a city telling a church that it was free to operate but not allowing the church access to city water, sewer, and electricity services, police and fire protection, and the use of city roads to and from the church. A U.S. appeals court upheld the university's position and the Supreme Court refused to hear the case.

Chapter 10

Christian Cleansing Via Abortions

*We hold these truths to be self-evident, that all men are cre-
ated equal, that they are endowed by their Creator with certain
unalienable Rights, that among these are Life, Liberty and the
pursuit of Happiness.* —Declaration of Independence

God who gave us life gave us liberty. Can the liberties of a nation
be secure when we have removed a conviction that these liberties are the gift of God? Indeed I tremble for my country when
I reflect that God is just, that His justice cannot sleep forever.
Commerce between master and slave is despotism. Nothing is
more certainly written in the book of fate than these people are
to be free. Establish the law for educating the common people.
This it is the business of the state to effect and on a general plan.
—Thomas Jefferson

Silence in the face of evil is itself evil: God will not hold us guilt-
less. Not to speak is to speak. Not to act is to act.
—Dietrich Bonhoeffer

For at least the last fifty years, liberals and progressives have tried to discredit the establishment of our country, the Declaration of Independence, the Constitution, and every principal held by conservatives, by tarring all our founding fathers as slave owners. While some of our founding fathers did own slaves, most of them decried slavery. The founding fathers certainly understood that people could not have the rights to liberty and pursue their idea of happiness unless they first had the right to live.

Evangelical Christians and most conservatives of various religious backgrounds believe in the sanctity of life. Life is sacred—all life. It doesn't matter if it is convenient to keep someone alive or not. The sacredness of life trumps all other considerations.

The intentional murder of unborn babies, called by the antiseptic and politically correct term of abortion, has led to the deaths of over 55 million babies since the 1973 Supreme Court decision in *Roe v. Wade.* These are babies that will never have birthdays, graduate from high school, hold jobs, get married, and have babies of their own. They have been denied the most basic of human rights: the right to live.

In *Men in Black: How the Supreme Court Is Destroying America,* Mark Levin reveals that the justices on the Supreme Court considered a number of things in ruling on *Roe v. Wade*—population control, the privacy rights of women, the role of abortion throughout world history, even popular opinion—but not the right of a baby in the womb to live.

Levin points out the fallacy of the ruling. Levin explains that the justices also didn't refer to or use the Constitution in their ruling on abortion. They instead viewed their ruling as a *policy* decision.

Although legislatures and governors have attempted to restrict or ban abortions in their particular state, their efforts have been largely ineffective. *Roe v. Wade* has been used by judges at every level to strike down those laws. A state law that simply requires a woman to have an ultrasound to show her that she is carrying a live baby, not a blob of cells, before she has an abortion is always challenged by pro-abortion groups ... and are almost always successful in overturning such laws, based on *Roe v. Wade*.

The March For Life held its fortieth rally in Washington, D.C., on January 25, 2013, and had a record attendance of over 500,000. While March For Life has raised awareness on the issue of abortion and has doubtless saved some lives, the hideous reality is that the murder of babies has become a lucrative business.

In January 2013, Planned Parenthood reported that they had performed a record number of abortions in 2012, abortions that were paid for with your tax dollars.

In its latest annual report for fiscal year 2011 to 2012, Planned Parenthood reveals that it performed 333,964 abortions in 2011—a record year for the organization. According to annual reports, the organization performed 332,278 abortions in 2009, 329,445 in 2010, making the total number of abortions in three years to 995,687. Planned Parenthood reported receiving a record $542 million in taxpayer funding, according to a Susan B. Anthony List analysis of the report, in the form of government grants, contracts, and Medicaid reimbursements. The amount is 45 percent of Planned Parenthood's annual revenue.

—WashingtonExaminer.com, January 7, 2013, "Planned Parenthood Reports Record Year for Abortions"

In 2011, the United States government's Centers for Disease Control reported that almost half the abortions performed in New York City involved black babies.

> In New York City in 2007, 87,527 abortions were performed, with 43,568—or 49.8 percent—of the aborted babies being black, according to the CDC. The number of white babies aborted in 2007 in New York City was 37,870—or 43.3 percent. 6,089, or 7 percent, were babies of other races, according to the report. According to the Census Bureau, there are 8,302,659 people in New York City, of whom 2,085,514—or 25 percent—are black. Thus, black babies in New York City were aborted at a rate that is twice the black share of the municipal population.
> —CNSNews.com, March 1, 2011, "Federal Report: Almost
> Half the Babies Aborted in NYC Were Black"

No one seems to bat an eye at the above statistics. But when pro-life groups unveiled billboards across the country with a picture of a cute, little black girl and the message, "The Most Dangerous Place for an African American Is in the Womb," it caused an uproar (NewsOne.com, October 15, 2010). When the billboard appeared in New York City, Christine Quinn, a member of the city council, had the gall to defend the murder of the unborn.

> To refer to a woman's legal right to an abortion as a "genocidal plot" is not only absurd, but it is offensive to women and to communities of color. Every woman deserves the right to make health care decisions for herself, and I will continue to fight to protect this basic right and against this sort of fear mongering.

Because abortion has been legal for so many years and has become such a part of our nation's culture, many Americans have no idea about the real history of abortion in the United States.

Margaret Sanger was born in 1879 and, according to her Wikipedia biography, she claimed to support birth control in order to save women from multiple pregnancies that led to health problems and death for women. In 1921, Sanger started the American Birth Control League, which eventually became the organization we know today as Planned Parenthood. Most people know nothing of Sanger's more controversial views on blacks or her involvement in eugenics. Below are just some of Sanger's statements which, for some reason, those who support Planned Parenthood have never revealed.

Colored people are like human weeds and are to be exterminated.   —*Pivot of Civilization*, 1922

Couples should be required to submit applications to have a child.   —*Birth Control Review*, April 1932

Organized charity itself is the symptom of a malignant social disease. Those vast, complex, interrelated organizations aiming to control and to diminish the spread of misery and destitution and all the menacing evils that spring out of this sinisterly fertile soil, are the surest sign that our civilization has bred, is breeding and perpetuating constantly increasing numbers of defectives, delinquents and dependents.   —BlackGenocide.org

It now remains for the U.S. government to set a sensible example to the world by offering a bonus or yearly pension to all obviously unfit parents who allow themselves to be *sterilized* by harmless and scientific means. In this way the moron and the diseased would have no posterity to inherit their unhappy condition. The number of the feeble-minded would decrease and a heavy burden would be lifted from the shoulders of the fit.

    —*Birth Control Review,* 1926, BlackGenocide.org

More children from the fit, less from the unfit—that is the chief aim of birth control.   —*Birth Control Review,* May 1919

The most merciful thing that a large family does to one of its infant members is to kill it.

    —*Women and the New Race,* Eugenics Publishing Co., 1923

Sanger worked to establish The Negro Project in 1939. The following quote is from a letter to Dr. Clarence Gamble that reveals her goals through this organization.

We should hire three or four colored ministers, preferably with social-service backgrounds, and with engaging personalities. The most successful educational approach to the Negro is through a religious appeal. We don't want the word to go out that we want to exterminate the Negro population. And the minister is the man who can straighten out that idea if it ever occurs to any of their more rebellious members.

    —www.nationalblackprolifeunion.com/Margaret-Sanger-and-
    The-Negro-Project.html, from *Woman's Body, Woman's Right:*
    A Social History of Birth Control in America, by Linda Gordo

Sanger also supported the Ku Klux Klan. In her 1939 autobiography, Sanger wrote:

> All the world over, in Penang and Skagway, in El Paso and Helsingfors, I have found women's psychology in the matter of childbearing essentially the same, no matter what the class, religion, or economic status. Always to me any aroused group was a good group, and therefore I accepted an invitation to talk to the women's branch of the Ku Klux Klan at Silver Lake, New Jersey, one of the weirdest experiences I had in lecturing.

Sanger said afterward that she felt the lecture had been a success and received a "dozen invitations to speak to similar groups."

While Planned Parenthood supports birth control, they just prefer to show that support through abortion. Margaret Sanger would be proud.

Because the murder of these precious babies is called by the sanitized term abortion, we rarely think about what an abortion actually entails. Life Site News, a pro-life website, gives the gruesome details on the many ways to murder a baby in the womb at the various stages of pregnancy. Some of these include suctioning the baby out, dismembering the baby with a special hook or knife, salt poisoning, or saline injection. Partial-birth abortion is particularly horrifying: the baby is part of the way out of the birth canal when a doctor jams a pair of scissors into the baby's skull. You can read more about the realities of abortion at www.lifesitenews.com/abortiontypes/.

Abortion also has long-term psychological, mental, and emotional effects for the mother. Actress and model Jennifer O'Neill had an abortion when she was only nineteen. After becoming a born-again Christian in 1986, O'Neill has become very involved with the pro-life movement. O'Neill wrote in her autobiography, *From Fallen To Forgiven*:

> I was told a lie from the pit of hell: that my baby was just a blob of tissue. The aftermath of abortion can be equally deadly for both mother and unborn child. A woman who has an abortion is sentenced to bear that for the rest of her life.

O'Neill recently told the *National Catholic Register*:

> Post-abortive women are prone to depression, suicide, alcohol and drug problems, and problems having relationships with later children.
>
> ... Whatever stage of gestation they're carrying their baby, there are people, organizations, and crisis-pregnancy centers all over the place that provide support, care and ultrasounds. Even among those who become pregnant through rape or incest, only one percent choose abortion. Most feel that violence was perpetrated against them, and they don't want to perpetrate violence against their child.

But O'Neill says that God can help and heal women who have had abortions. "God had a plan for my life; he was waiting for me to turn to him. It's been a journey of repair, renewal, and revival."

No one knows the healing power of God from an abortion more than Charlie and Linda Meadows. Charlie is the co-founder and president of the Oklahoma Conservative Political Action

Committee or OCPAC. Sometimes at their weekly meetings, Charlie will challenge a local politician's stand on allowing abortion in cases of rape or incest by asking, "What did that baby do to deserve death?" Some people would criticize Charlie for daring to oppose abortion in cases of rape or incest unless they knew the story behind that question. When she was a young girl, Linda was raped by a family member and became pregnant. Linda's parents decided to take the situation into their own hands, and they performed an abortion on Linda in their home.

Charlie and Linda are living examples of how God's grace and love can triumph in tragic situations. They were able to forgive the family member who raped Linda, and Linda is now volunteering at a local pro-life pregnancy clinic. A politician or a conservative is often attacked for opposing abortion in any circumstance. The Meadows experienced the unimaginable and, in spite of everything, they made the decision to support life.

Unfortunately, President Obama is our country's most pro-abortion president. When he was a state senator in Illinois, President Obama voted against a bill that would allow a baby who had survived an abortion to receive life-saving care. When he was campaigning for president in 2008, President Obama said he would not want his two daughters "to be punished with a baby." Through Obamacare, President Obama is forcing Christians, conservatives, and anyone else opposed to abortion to pay for pills that terminate pregnancies. His attorney general is using the Obamacare law to take Christians who own private businesses and oppose paying for the "morning after" abortion pill through their employee health care plans to court.

When God condemned the nations surrounding Israel, one of

the reasons He did so was because they sacrificed their children to their pagan gods.

> And thou shalt not let any of thy seed pass through the fire to Molech, neither shalt thou profane the name of thy God.
>
> —Leviticus 18:21

> There shall not be found among you any one that maketh his son or his daughter to pass through the fire, or that useth divination, or an observer of times, or an enchanter, or a witch. Or a charmer, or a consulter with familiar spirits, or a wizard, or a necromancer. For all that do these things are an abomination unto the LORD: and because of these abominations the LORD thy God doth drive them out from before thee.
>
> —Deuteronomy 18:10–12

The United States has earned God's judgment for its refusal to end its policy of abortion on demand. We certainly cannot prosper as a nation unless or until we repent.

> ### Forget Abortion! NPR Promotes The "Rights" and "Souls" of Plants

(Newsbusters.com, October 28, 2012)—This article quotes Linton Weeks, who believes that plants and vegetables have rights. Tim Graham, the reporter, points out how hypocritical it is to promote the rights of vegetables while denying the rights of babies conceived from rape and the mentally-incapacitated, like Terry Schiavo, to live. This is one more article which demonstrates how far our country has deteriorated when people defend the rights of weeds but not the rights of human beings.

> **491 Babies Born Alive After Failed Abortions, Left to Die: Statistics Canada Confirms**
>
> (LifeSiteNews.com, November 28, 2012)—President Barack Obama voted against saving the lives of babies who had survived abortions when he served in the Illinois state senate. Although this news item is about what is happening in Canada, it illustrates the point of the heartlessness of those who support abortion.

> **Selective-Sex Abortion Bill Re-Ignites Women's Rights Debate**
>
> (*U.S. News & World Report,* May 31, 2012)—Women in Great Britain are having abortions based on the sex of the baby. It is horrifying that this is also now happening in the United States. Arizona Representative Trent Franks said that this practice is widespread in our country so he introduced the Prenatal Nondiscrimination Act. It is shameful that although Republicans have a majority in the House of Representatives, the bill failed, 246–168.

> **NYC Schools Hand Out 12,721 "Morning-After" Pills**
>
> (*Washington Times,* February 3, 2013)—Many schools no longer allow cupcakes and candy at school parties, or candy bars and potato chips in school vending machines, but they freely hand out abortion pills to students without the permission of the student's parents! Of course, city officials refused to discuss the practice. Thankfully, the president of the NYC Parents Union was shocked and blasted New York City mayor Michael Bloomberg. Nothing will probably change in New

York City schools, but it is alarming that this practice is probably going on in your child's school without your notice.

Chapter 11

Christian Cleansing in the Church

On an individual church basis, organizations like the National Council of Churches and the World Council of Churches, including denominational and doctrinal church affiliations, have not brought Christians, or church members, together in any spiritual or political sense.

The Baptist church on one corner teaches that if you have it, you can't lose; the Pentecostal church on the next corner teaches that if you have it, you might lose it. Most churches meet once on Wednesday and twice on Sunday, while the "what a difference a day makes" church teaches that you must worship on Saturday or you have taken the mark of the beast. The Catholic churches are resisting political efforts to force the authority of President Obama over the pope in Rome while still having problems with pedophile priests.

Nine out of ten local pastors do not care what is happening in Washington, Moscow, Jerusalem, or the United Nations. They are ninety-nine percent interested in how many were in attendance last Sunday, what the offering was, and if at the next deacons' meeting he will be invited to continue as pastor for another year. We wonder why pastors today are seemingly hiding behind their pulpits with a 501(c)3 message instead of breathing fire and brimstone like Dwight L. Moody and Billy Sunday. Why are there not some like Elijah who pointed his finger at Ahab and Jezebel and charged, "You have made Israel to sin"?

In the Revolutionary War for independence, a black robed regiment of preachers encouraged the regular army, and since that time, when there have been moral, spiritual, economic, or military crises, for the most part pastors have taken an active role in supporting the nation's needs. The evangelical Christians were given credit for electing Ronald Reagan to the office of president twice.

In 2012, the number of citizens who voted was 18 million less than in 2008, partially because many Christians stayed home rather than vote for a Mormon. Of those Christians that did vote, a large percentage voted for Obama, a pro-homosexual president.

According to the *2011 World Almanac,* of the some 300 million population of the United States, fifty-one percent are Protestant; Roman Catholic, twenty-four percent; Mormon, two percent; other Christians, two percent; Jewish, two percent; and no religious affiliation, four percent. The *World Almanac* did not mention what the remaining fifteen percent believed. Perhaps this is prison and mental institution populations, or non-adults. These statistics indicate that ninety-six out of one hundred Americans belong to some church or religious entity, yet 40 million of the last 80 million babies born in the United States were born out of wedlock.

The president of the United States announced the government

would no longer recognize the union of one man and one woman as the only legal marriage; state after state are also now defining marriage as a union of two men or two women.

Jesus said that as it was at Sodom and Gomorrah, so it would be when He came again. The Apostle Paul explains in Romans 1 that homosexuality is perhaps the greatest scourge of the human race. Yet, our president says that homosexuals are the best citizens we have in America for government service. He also said that this was no longer considered a Christian nation when seventy-seven percent of the U.S. population belongs to a Christian church.

Inasmuch as many agree that the homosexual issue, a pet project of the Obama administration, is the most serious issue facing the churches today in a collective sense, and also to Christians individually, the following headline stories are submitted for your consideration:

> **Why No Denomination Will Survive the Homosexual Crisis**
> (ChristianPost.com, July 18, 2012)—An opinion that the homosexual issue will further divide conservative and pro-gay liberal church members. The conservatives will lose and leave, leaving church memberships either gay or pro-gay, and thousands of churches will close.

> **Faith Leaders Endorse Gay Marriage Law**
> (ChristianPost.com, December 26, 2012)—Over 250 pastors and rabbis in Illinois give their support for a law making gay marriage as legal as that of a marriage between one man and one woman.

> **The Queen James Bible**
> (TheGospelCoalition.org, December 16, 2012)—A new edi-

tion of the Bible for gays, or churches that accept gays, which takes out all references to homosexuality, including the reason for Sodom's destruction. This gay Bible may be the main Bible for churches in the future.

> **Church Compromising on Bible Truth**
> (OneNewsNow.com, August 16, 2011)—Many churches, including Willow Creek in Chicago, are no longer encouraging homosexuals to change, but rather they accept them as all other members—average, normal church members.

> **Selection of Gay Leader**
> (OneNewsNow.com, December 29, 2010)—The North Carolina Council of Churches elected Stan Kimer, an open, practicing homosexual, to be president.

> **Church Billboard: Was Jesus Gay**
> (Aukland—LocalNews.com, December 19, 2012)—A Christmas billboard shows the Baby Jesus in His crib of rainbow colors.

The preceding news stories are only a small percentage of those relating to the church/homosexual issue that passes over our desks. Most pastors today try to ignore the issue, hoping that it will just go away and not become an issue they will have to confront. One question they will be asked at the Judgment Seat of Christ is, "Did you contend for the faith once delivered to the saints?"

A recent news item in *Christian News* reports that Christians are being arrested in New Orleans for witnessing on the streets after sundown. Other items report that Christians are being arrested in malls for witnessing. Still other Christian news publications report that tithing is down, and the Southern Baptist Convention reports a sharp decline in church membership.

A Media Research Center news report dated December 13, 2012, reports: "Tis the season to censor the free expression of religion. ... The American left's fanatical obsession with purging any mention of Christianity from the public square is intensifying. ..."

Other news items report that homosexuals are now being considered for membership, and even leadership roles, in the Boy Scouts, something that most believe will destroy the Boy Scouts of America. It is unimaginable that a possible pedophilic homosexual could be turned loose on a group of eight-year-old Boy Scouts.

The church at large should be addressing these issues and problems that confront the future of the freedom of religion and dangers to Christian faith and worship. But it is not. Most church members listen to their pastors for twenty minutes on Sunday, but they watch television and listen to the news media twenty hours a week. The news media, in general, is anti-Christian. More Americans listen to Oprah Winfrey during the week than go to church on Sunday.

The anti-Christian movement is not just in the United States, as we have previously referenced, but is worldwide. A December 5, 2012, article from OneNewsNow.com reports that while homosexuals are now being considered for membership in the Boy Scouts of America, both the Girl Scouts and Boy Scouts of Great Britain have been ordered to admit atheists.

Another OneNewsNow.com article dated March 2, 2011, reports that a Christian couple were denied to foster children because they do not approve of homosexuality.

Christian schools in Canada will be closed unless they teach evolution in their science classes. In Texas, a judge recently fined a mother and took her daughter because she spanked her daughter with her hand. In Ireland, the government has ruled that the rights of children exceed parental authority. *The London Telegraph* reported on February 22, 2012, the government has told Christians that when the law is contrary to Christian faith and beliefs, Christians must obey the government or go to jail. On March 3, 2011, the government informed parents in Germany that they would go to jail if they withheld their children from sex education classes. In England and most of Europe, new euthanasia laws are being passed to give the government the right to end the lives of children and the mentally ill.

Perhaps the largest so-called Christian cleansing effort in the church was the Purpose Driven movement by Dr. Rick Warren. The idea behind the PDC effort was that the church was not reaching the younger generation or the general unsaved public. Dr. Warren wrote every household in Orange County, California, asking them to respond as to what kind of church they would attend. It can be imagined what kind of church the vast majority of the unsaved who responded would attend. However, Dr. Warren modeled his church, Saddleback, on the basis of the response to his letter.

Crosses and other Christian identification was removed; the music was changed to a loud secular type of music; brighter colors for the church came later; and sermon contents and length were changed to please the impatient audience in a hurry to get home and watch the afternoon football game. Dr. Warren's church model soon attracted more than 25,000 members. At the same time, Zondervan Publishing released a book entitled *The Purpose Driven Life* that supposedly invited carnal or unstable Christians into a happier and more successful lifestyle. It was written to sell, and it did—by the millions—also adding to the reputation of the rising Purpose Driven Church. Membership was stressed instead of salvation by faith, and the solemn church music and order was changed to a more entertaining type of service and outreach. Dr. Warren ignored the advice by Charles Spurgeon that the biggest lie the devil ever told was that churches could win souls with entertainment.

My own church, Council Road Baptist Church of Oklahoma City, was one of the larger churches in the Southern Baptist Convention, with an attendance of several thousand. There was a change in leadership in 2004 that converted to the Purpose Driven Church order of worship. The membership left by the thousands, and it was then that I wrote *The Dark Side of the Purpose Driven Church* and a related tract, "Has Your Church Gone Purpose Driven? How Can You Tell?"

The book and tract have been useful across the nation in saving many churches that were going Purpose Driven. The pastor of the First Baptist Church of Daytona Beach, an important church in the SBC, announced to the world that I was "ignorant, mentally ill, and un-Christian." The church didn't think so, and after a vote on a Wednesday evening, the *Baptist Press* carried a front-page headline: "Dr. Cox Resigns."

Dr. Warren is a member of the Council on Foreign Relations and appears at important U.N. and U.S.A. functions. He also gets involved in trying to decide moral and personal relationship standards in other nations, which at times is not appreciated. The Uganda National Task Force Against Homosexuality in 2010 was trying to save the nation from the ravages of AIDS that are rampant in equatorial Africa.

The taskforce represents

> **The National Fellowship of Born-again Churches**
> **The Seventh Adventists Church**
> **The Uganda Joint Christian Council which also represents:**
>   » The Orthodox Church in Uganda
>   » The Roman Catholic Church in Uganda
>   » The Islamic Office of Social Welfare in Uganda
>   » Born Again Faith Federation
>   » familypolicycenter@gmail.com

Dear Rick Warren,

Christmas greetings from the Pro Faith, Family, and Human Rights Leaders here in Uganda. We acknowledge receipt of a letter from you in which you called on us (Ugandan Pastors) to "speak out" against the proposed "Anti–homosexuality Bill 2009" which is currently before our parliament. This bill has been greatly misrepresented by some homosexual activists causing hysteria and we take this opportunity to give you the background, facts and response to the concerns you raised. A special meeting of 20 denominational heads met on Thursday 17th Dec. in the offices of the minister of Ethics and Integrity, examined your letter and formed a joint task force to respond to you as well as help support the parliament in the passage of this bill. We are further distressed by your unwarranted abuse of our duly elected officials who are in the process of making laws in the fulfillment of their mission and make demand that you biblically issue an apology for having wronged us as demonstrated by the facts of this letter.

Developments underlying the Bill

Several developments in Uganda and around the world constitute the compelling circumstances that have necessitated the
Anti-homosexuality Bill. These include:

1. Increasing incidents of homosexual abuse of children and
   youth by people exercising power and influence over them
   like teachers, pastors, parents, etc. A recent report shows
   this.

2. Recruitment of youth into homosexual practice with
   inducements including money. While we have a law that
   currently prohibits "acts against the order of nature," this
   law is not comprehensive enough to cover the promoters of
   these acts. The draft law seeks to stop promotion and further recruitment of unsuspecting children and youth into
   homosexuality.

3. Promotion of homosexuality by some organizations,
   including a pro-gay book by UNICEF circulated in schools
   without seeking permission of the Ministry of Education.

4. Creation of organizations whose sole purpose is to promote
   homosexuality in Uganda.

5. Government-led campaigns at the UN led by some countries like France and Brazil to secure a UN General Assem-
   bly resolution imposing homosexuality as an internationally
   protected human right. For example, on November 18th
   2008, France and Netherlands initiated a law which seeks to
   use the UN to push homosexuality on other nations of the
   world. This explains provisions in the Bill preventing ratifi-
   cation of treaties and conventions affirming homosexuality
   and related practices.

6. Unbelievable growth in the power of the homosexual lobby in western countries, clearly seen since this Bill was proposed in Uganda—entire governments in Europe and America have used their diplomatic offices on an issue that should be freely debated and dealt with by their citizens at civil society level.

7. The mistake in western society, where the issue of homo-sexuality was treated with kid gloves as a minor, private issue, but these societies are waking up too late on realiz-ing that the matter affects how their entire society is ran, what children are taught at school and literally what every-body "must believe and practice." This waking-up is for example seen in anti-gay-marriage campaigns in United States, where US citizens are fighting to retain family val-ues against stiff competition from gay activists in 31 states where the matter has come up for a referendum vote, win-ning such battles by the skin of their teeth. These countries are stuck with a huge population of their citizens that has been recruited into homosexual practice over decades of lax attitude that has seen the rise of powerful, well-funded organizations that misinform children and youth about homosexuality and daily recruit them into their ranks. This discontented population is angry, a threat to public order and is demanding equality for self-evident disordered and harmful behavior. This represents a mismanagement of human behavior by public institutions, because legal safe-guards were not put in place in time to prevent the spread of homosexuality and related practices.

8. The takeover by homosexuals of western institutions that

should have remained as defenders and protectors of moral integrity in society, particularly the church, to the extent that even evangelical church leaders in America no longer protest when a practicing homosexual is appointed into pastoral leadership in the church (e.g. the election to the office of Bishop of Mary Glasspool in your state of California last week and Gene Robinson in New Hampshire before her). This institutional takeover by homosexuals has been systematic and planned, to the extent that other bodies like the UN, national governments, financial institutions, private companies, NGOs, etc. have become spokespersons of the gay movement and daily use official resources to promote the gay agenda and to arm-twist anyone who opposes this agenda. In a globalized world, this western takeover of institutions by homosexuals has turned into international promotion of homosexuality and of other vices like abortion and pornography in other countries.

9. Some members of Parliament in Uganda have looked at all these developments as a threat to strongly held family values in Uganda and everywhere and have sought to use their mandate as people's representatives to seek remedies before it is too late. The Anti-homosexuality Bill 2009, therefore, while acknowledging that homosexuality is not an innate condition, states as its object: "to establish a comprehensive consolidated legislation to protect the traditional family by prohibiting (1) any form of sexual relations between persons of the same sex; and (2) the promotion or recognition of such sexual relations in public institutions and other places through or with the support of any Government

entity in Uganda or any non-governmental organization inside or outside the country".

What's the death penalty all about?

Some people have asked about the rationale of a death penalty mentioned in the Bill. There has been a lot of misinformation about this matter with headlines such as: "Gays face death penalty in Uganda." These headlines are deliberately misleading. This penalty applies only in special cases termed "aggravated homosexuality," which include, those convicted of unlawful homosexual rape of a child or handicapped invalid; This is a conviction of pedophiles! As highlighted in the problem of "virgin rape cures HIV/AIDS" the offender can be a person living with HIV; a parent or guardian of the victim where there is abuse of authority! Finally is the use of drugs to stupefy the child so that they can rape them! Clearly, the intent of this penalty is to protect weaker members of society from being victimized. Please note that for over 15 years Uganda has had the same penalty for persons who have carnal knowledge of minors heterosexually, mainly to protect against sexual abuse of girls by men. This time, this provision intends to provide equal protection of boys, among others.

In the early 1990s, at the height of the HIV Crisis, Uganda sought to protect children, principally girls, from sexual abuse by adults and infection with HIV. There was troubling concern over some people living with HIV/AIDS (PLWA) who raped and infected girls with HIV/AIDS in a grotesque belief of a "virgin sex cure" prescribed by some witchdoctors. Since 1997, Section 123 of the Penal Code only provided protection against defilement (sexual abuse) of girls under 18 years of age. Section 123(1) states that: "Any person who unlawfully has sexual intercourse with a girl under the age of eighteen years is guilty of an offense and is liable to suffer death." Sub-section 2 of Section 123 of the Penal Code provides for attempts to defile a girl under the age of eighteen years. It states that: "Any person who attempts to have unlawful sexual intercourse with a girl under the age of eighteen years is guilty of an offense and is liable to imprisonment for eighteen years with or without corporal punishment." This has and continues to be the law which no one has complained that it is unchristian or a human right violation. Many boys have been violated without legal protection leaving their evil oppressors to get away with no law enforcement protection. The current draft law simply aims at providing equal protection of the boy child and other vulnerable persons, as currently exists for the girl child. The question for you is this: does the sexual abuse of a boy constitute a lesser crime than the rape of a girl?

The question of human rights and privacy

Some people have asked whether this law raises questions of human rights infringement. Some have asked whether it infringes the right to privacy, for example, asking what legitimate interest the state has in what people do in the privacy of their bedrooms? But not all things done in private are free of negative consequences on the public. Most harmful behavior occurs in private: corruption, bribery, abortion, murder, rape, etc. Many laws prohibit these private practices. Practices like homosexuality and bisexuality are associated with serious, yet preventable public-health risks. The risk of HIV transmission in male homosexuality is for example about 10 times that of heterosexual sex, simply due to use of parts of the body for inappropriate functions. Other diseases and medical complications are also associated with these practices. Secondly, by its nature, behavior spreads in the population through experimentation, modeling and social affirmation. Increase in homosexual and bisexual practice could thus rapidly reverse Uganda's success against HIV/AIDS. The state's interest in public health requires that it takes action on these preventable health risks, not only through education, but also legal deterrents for those who misinform and mislead the public.

An organization recruiting and encouraging people to continue in homosexual practice lacks justification but one dealing in counseling and helping people with behavior management is justified. The clause requiring mandatory reporting of known offenses may therefore need an amendment to exempt disclosure made in counseling situations.

Our Historical Struggle

When you [Rick Warren] came to Uganda on Thursday, 27 March 2008, and expressed support to the Church of Uganda's boycott of the pro-homosexual Church of England, you stated; "The Church of England is wrong, and I support the Church of Uganda." You are further remembered to say, "homosexuality is not a natural way of life and thus [its] not a human right. We shall not tolerate this aspect at all" (Gay Row, US Pastor supports country on boycott). He was indeed affirming Uganda's long historical struggle against institutionalized homosexuality.

This recent boycott was not the beginning of the struggle. In fact on June 3rd 1886, 26 Ugandan Christian converts were martyred for their stand against a deviant king who had taken to the practice of sodomy. Their faith in Christ emboldened them to stand against homosexuality, resisting even up to death. Today we honor them, and June 3rd is a national holiday where millions of Ugandan believers converge to remember and renew their strength. As you yourself have said, ". . . the Bible says evil has to be opposed. Evil has to be stopped. The Bible does not say negotiate with evil. It says stop it. Stop evil" (December 2007). Since homosexuality is evil, you cannot possibly be against a law that seeks to stop it unless you have misunderstood it.

Clarification on the spirit of the mandatory reporting clause 14
Finally, sexual abuse of children takes place in institutions such as boarding schools, churches etc. Research by ACFODE, "The situational review of rape, sexual harassment and defilement 2005" in three districts found unusually high levels of coercive heterosexual/homosexual rape and harassment especially in single-sex schools. Unfortunately the school officials and some police officers maintain a conspiracy of silence, ignoring the pleas of the children and victims who report these crimes. They value the reputation of the school or other institution above the welfare of the children and adults in their custody. This is the reason for section 14, of mandatory reporting of the offenses within 24 hours.

This reporting is similar to the mandatory reporting of all "unlawful sexual intercourse" in the state of California in Penal Code 11165 which includes, rape (261), incest (285), sodomy

(286), child molestation (647.6), and statutory rape (261.5). California Penal Code 11166; 11165.7 requires that Teachers, Social workers, District attorneys, Doctors, Psychologists, marriage and family counselors, clergy members and state or county public health employees are required by law to report "unlawful sexual intercourse" as defined by the state of California. If mandatory reporting has been deemed necessary in America on sexual offenses, Uganda could use the same measure in specified situations.

What has been our recommendation on the law?

At a special sitting of the Uganda Joint Christian Council a taskforce sat and reviewed the bill to make comments. We resolved to support the bill with some amendments which included the following:

1. We suggested reduction of the sentence to 20 years instead of the death penalty for the offense of aggravated homosexuality.

2. We suggested the inclusion of regulations in the law to govern provision of counseling and rehabilitation to persons experiencing homosexual temptations. The churches are willing to provide the necessary help for those seeking counseling and rehabilitation.

3. Even with the provision for counseling and rehabilitation in the law, homosexuality should remain a punishable offense to control its spread.

Warning of a widening shift

We note with sadness the increasing levels of accepting of the evil of homosexuality. The ordination of Mary Glasspool a Lesbian as a bishop in Los Angeles without any condemnation from you, has increased the widening gap between the global south church in Africa and the global north church in Europe and America. In these increasingly dark days, we encourage you not to give into the temptation to water down what the Bible says so as not to offend people. Jesus's gospel is a stumbling block, and a rock of offense. Rick you are our friend, we have bought many of your books and have been blessed by them. Do not let the pressure of bloggers and popular media intimidate you into becoming a negotiator for homosexual pedophilia rights in Africa. As you yourself say about evil, "the Bible says evil has to be opposed. Evil has to be stopped. The Bible does not say negotiate with evil. It says stop it. Stop evil." Since the Bible says that the giant of homosexuality is an "abomination" or a great evil, you cannot achieve the peace plan without a purpose driven confrontation with evil.

Ugandan Clergy Demand for your apology within

Please note that on Friday 11th December, more than 200 of Uganda's top religious leaders met and supported the legislators in strengthening the law against homosexuality. The issue is, we all want the law on homosexuality, the only debate is on what penalties are appropriate.

Your letter has caused great distress and the pastors are demanding that you issue a formal apology for insulting the people of Africa by your very inappropriate bully use of your church and purpose driven pulpits to coerce us into the "evil" of Sodomy and Gaymorrah. This is expected within seven days from this date.

Sincerely Yours,

Martin Ssempa, Phd

Bishop David Kiganda

Pastor Ssozi Peter

Prof. Peter Claver Matovu

Seventh Day Church Representative.

familypolicycenter@gmail.com

We included the full text of the Uganda anti-homosexual legislation with the support of Ugandan churches, along with their clear response to Dr. Rick Warren, for several reasons:

1. The bill explains the role the United Nations has in promoting homosexual immorality into all nations through its agencies like UNICEF.
2. The horrendous results of homosexuality unchecked and unopposed by the churches, spreading death-killing AIDS and ruining the lives of young boys and girls.
3. The insidious dangers of apostasy infiltrating the churches through the Purpose Driven Church movement weakening the biblical doctrines of the Gospel to oppose homosexuality and other sins that are destroying the United States of America.

The latest controversy associated with the Purpose Driven Church is that Dr. Warren has been promoting interfaith meetings of Christians and Muslims at Saddleback and teaching a doctrine of Chrislam—that Christians and Muslims worship the same God. Having not attended any of these sessions, I cannot say how much credibility is behind the charges, but I would assume there is some.

From taking hundreds of telephone calls at my office, it seems to me that the Purpose Driven Church movement has destroyed far more fundamental churches than it has helped, if it has helped any. It has caused dissension between brethren, and is at least a major part of the falling away of the church and Christian faith as prophesied for the last days.

The Christian cleansing process in the family, school, government, and state and federal institutions, is having its united effects:

> **Massive Number of U.S. Cities Abandon Bible**
> (WorldNetDaily.com, January 31, 2013)—Providence, Rhode Island, named in respect and belief in God's divine providence, is now named to be the least Bible-honoring city in the United States. In ninety-six of our major cities less than twenty percent of the population own a Bible.

> **Obama condemns rights of Christian military chaplains**
> (OneNewsNow.com, January 9, 2013)—The president strongly condemned Army and Navy chaplains for wanting to not have to marry homosexuals in military service.

> **Anti-religious groups not done with West Point**
> (OneNewsNow.com, January 15, 2013)—The Separation of Church and State organization will sue West Point Military Academy if it continues invocations at assemblies.

> **What Religious Freedom?**
> (ChristianPost.com, January 24, 2013)—President Obama has declared January 16 to be "Religious Freedom Day," for all religions to express their faith in their gods, but Christians are commanded to witness every day that Jesus Christ came

to save those who are lost in sin.

> ### God May Bring America "To Its Knees," Says Disappointed Franklin Graham

(ChristianPost.com, November 19, 2012)—Dr. Franklin Graham expressed serious concerns that more Christians did not vote in the last presidential election and that the church had lost its presence in the affairs of the state. He believes there will be an economic collapse before revival can come.

Many Christians pray for revival in America, but the Christian cleansing movement in our nation within the government, schools, news media, and even some denominations has left in its wake a church seriously in need of revival. However, a revival must come from the pulpits of the land, but only an era of Christian persecution as happened in Russia, China, and now the Middle East, can bring that about. The vast majority of pastors are satisfied with their jobs and the spiritual condition of their own congregations. But the church in America will continue to have troubles that will get even worse, as we have referenced in this book.

If my people, which are called by my name, shall humble themselves, and pray, and seek my face, and turn from their wicked ways; then will I hear from heaven, and will forgive their sin, and will heal their land.   —2 Chronicles 7:14

Chapter 12

Christian Cleansing via Obamacare

Unless we put medical freedom into the Constitution the time will come when medicine will organize itself into an undercover dictatorship. To restrict the art of healing to doctors and deny equal privileges to others will constitute the Bastille of medical science. All such laws are un-American and despotic.

—Dr. Benjamin Rush, signer of the
Declaration of Independence

The Patient Protection and Affordable Care Act, known as Obamacare, is one of the most direct and vicious attacks on Americans, and especially Christians, in the history of our nation. The federal government in 2012 had already issued 70,000 pages of regulations and rules for the implementation of the Obamacare law. The dramatic increase in health insurance premiums for Americans, twenty-one new taxes (including a new tax on medical devices), and the expansion of Medicaid that will eventually bankrupt the states that accept it—as bad as these three provisions are—are not the worst of what is in the Obamacare law.

Abortion Pills, Contraceptives, and Sterilizations: When Obamacare was passed, the bill had many blank spaces for rules which were to be decided later by the secretary of Health and Human Services. HHS secretary Kathleen Sebelius, a former governor of Kansas, is a strong pro-abortionist, which has had an influence on the rules she has issued for the Obamacare law. One of Sebelius' rules forces taxpayers and private companies to pay for health insurance plans that include abortions, the morning-after abortion pill, contraceptives, and sterilizations for women. While religious organizations are exempt (for now), Christians and others who own private companies and businesses and who are opposed to abortion and sterilization for religious reasons are not.

The Heritage Foundation documented this in a March 7, 2012, article on their website, "The 10 Terrible Provisions of Obamacare You May Not Have Heard Of."

> The Department of Health and Human Services included the full range of contraceptives, including abortion-inducing drugs, among the women-specific preventive services that Obamacare requires insurers to include with no cost-sharing. This mandate violates Americans' conscience rights and religious liberty. Its narrow exemption for religious employers will force many who find these products morally objectionable—including religious charities, hospitals, and schools—to pay for them.

This is why a number of businesses like Hobby Lobby, owned by the Green family, who are evangelical Christians, and Christy

Industries, owned by Catholic Frank O'Brien, have filed lawsuits against the Obamacare law on the basis that the above mandates violate their First Amendment rights to religious liberty. Most expect this lawsuit to go all the way to the Supreme Court.

One of the most disturbing things covered in the above Obamacare mandate is the forced coverage of sterilizations. CNSNews.com documented this mandate in an article on March 17, 2012, "Free Sterilizations Must Be Offered to All College Women, Says HHS."

> Women of college age who do not attend school will also get free sterilization coverage whether they are insured through an employer, their parents, or some form of government-subsidized plan. ... These free "preventive services" include surgical sterilization procedures and all Food and Drug Administration-approved contraceptives, including those that cause abortions.

The idea of sterilizing young women so that they could never have children ostensibly came from the Institute of Medicine (part of the National Academy of Sciences) which is funded by your tax dollars. Why would our government encourage the sterilization of women?

Because of the objections and approximately forty lawsuits of so many religious organizations and individuals against this portion of the Obamacare mandate, HHS Secretary Sebelius came out with an "accommodation," but it was rejected by Christian and religious organizations as a farce. The CNSNews.com article on February 1, 2013, "Obama Administration: We Will Still Force Christians to Act Against Their Faith," detailed the future fight.

The Department of Health and Human Services on Friday set the stage for a massive showdown between the federal government of the United States and American Christians who believe the government has no right to force them to act against their faith by mandating that they buy, provide or facilitate healthcare coverage that includes sterilizations, contraception, or abortion-inducing drugs.

Maureen Ferguson, senior policy advisor to The Catholic Association, said:

The HHS mandate announcement today changes nothing, it is just another accounting gimmick and the HHS mandate continues to be a violation of civil rights, religious freedom and First Amendment rights. … Catholic institutions and other faith based organizations, including hospitals and universities and private employers, still do not get their First Amendment rights back and are still being forced to either violate their faith or pay crippling government fines for practicing their faith.

Marriage and Families: According to The Heritage Foundation article, "The 10 Terrible Provisions of Obamacare You May Not Have Heard Of," Obamacare penalizes marriages and therefore families.

Obamacare creates new taxpayer-funded subsidies for the low and middle classes to purchase health coverage, but the structure of the subsidies allows two individuals to claim more in subsidies alone than if married. This discriminates against married couples and discourages marriage at almost all age and income levels.

Marriages and families are the basic foundation of any society. A CNSNews.com article on February 12, 2013, underscores this in "Intact Families—Not Government Social Programs—Most Beneficial to Children and Society, Group Finds."

> Children raised by their married, biological mother and father have better lives and rely less on government programs, a pair of studies by a family advocacy group finds. The Index of Family Belonging and Rejection measured the number of children being raised by their married parents in U.S. cities and states, and the report, "U.S. Social Policy: Dependence on the Family," correlated those statistics with dependence on government social programs like food stamps and welfare.

Patrick Fagan, director of the Family Research Council's Marriage and Religion Research Institute (MARRI), said that "with what he calls the 'retreat of marriage' in modern society, scholars and others realize anew that the institutions of marriage and family are cornerstones of Western civilization."

The article quoted the study, "The state has hitherto ignored the importance of the intact married family in shaping the outcomes of its social policies. This neglect of marriage is an error of historical proportions."

The Obamacare law is, without a doubt, a direct attack on the God-established institution of marriage and the family.

Death Panels: Democrats attacked Sarah Palin for saying that

Obamacare contained death panels. But The Heritage Foundation article, "The 10 Terrible Provisions of Obamacare You May Not Have Heard Of" verifies the establishment of the Independent Payment Advisory Board. "The Independent Payment Advisory Board, a board of 15 unelected officials, will have the power to cut Medicare spending without congressional approval. These unaccountable government appointees will be able to restrict seniors' access to providers, treatments, and services."

It is not surprising that with all the negative publicity surrounding the IPAB panel that the Obama administration is having trouble finding people who will serve on it. Both TheBlaze.com and *The Washington Post* have reported that even Jonathan Gruber, who played important roles in both Romneycare in Massachusetts and Obamacare, has flatly refused to be on IPAB.

TheBlaze.com article, "Guess What: Obama's Having A Hard Time Finding Anyone To Serve On That So-Called 'Death Panel'" on January 28, 2013, listed some of the reasons why people aren't interested in being on IPAB. The position is full-time for six years; the pay is limited; you cannot work outside of serving on IPAB; and you must first qualify and then go through confirmation hearings.

If you are having to make life-and-death decisions over people, it is obvious that those decisions are not going to be popular. Would you want to be on a board like that?

Seniors: Accuracy in Media held a conference on September 21, 2012, "Obamanation: A Day of Truth." One of the speakers was Betsy McCaughey, who has written extensively on the Obamacare law. The title of her talk was "Scientific Evidence Proves Obamacare Will Harm Seniors." A video and transcript of her talk is still on the Accuracy in Media website at http://www.aim.org/video/

betsy-mccaughey-scientific-evidence-proves-obamacare-will-harm-seniors/.

McCaughey says that the "cuts to hospitals, and doctors, and hospice care, and dialysis centers, and home care—the cuts under the Obama health law to the providers of care to seniors are so severe that the Obama health law destroyed Medicare. Eviscerated it. You haven't felt the effects yet, but you will soon. The only thing left of Medicare is the membership card."

McCaughey predicts many unnecessary deaths in hospitals from the Obamacare law rules.

> Soon you will begin to see the changes in hospitals: The emergence of an environment of scarcity. Fewer nurses on the floor. Waits for MRIs. Less physical therapy available. Less room cleaning. The Obama health law takes $247 billion out of future funding for payments to hospitals over the next decade. Hospitals will have $247 billion less to care for the same number of seniors. Now the President says—and he'll say it today again at AARP—"Don't worry, I'm only cutting payments to providers, I'm not cutting benefits for seniors." Don't be bamboozled! It's a trick. It's an illusion. The fact is that Medicare already pays less than the actual cost of care to a hospital—91 cents for every dollar of care delivered. So when the payments to hospitals are cut, it's not going to trim hospital profit margins—they're already in the negative! It's going to force hospitals to deliver less care.

McCaughey continues:

> These cuts in what hospitals are paid to care for seniors will worsen the chance that elderly patients survive their hospital

stay, and recover. … The *Annals of Internal Medicine,* a very prestigious medical journal, published, in 2011, the data showing that elderly patients treated in low-spending hospitals had a substantially worse chance of recovering from their illnesses than patients of exactly the same age, with the same diagnosis, the same illness, treated at a higher spending hospital. For example, elderly patients who went to the hospital with a heart attack were 19% more likely to die from it in a low-spending hospital than in a high-spending hospital; in the high-spending hospital they had a better shot at recovering and leaving the hospital.

At the time of her talk, McCaughey revealed what has now taken place under the Obamacare law directly impacting seniors.

In just a few days, October 2012, the Obama administration will start awarding "bonus points" to the hospitals that spend the least per senior. Oh, yes! Section 3001 of this law, for the first time, creates a new "quality measure for Medicare." It measures spending per Medicare beneficiary, and awards the bonus points to the hospitals that spend the least per senior! And it whacks the higher spending hospitals with demerits, not only for what they spend on a patient while the patient is in the hospital, but also what is spent on that patient for the three months after hospitalization. So hospitals also get hit with demerits for recommending physical therapy after the patient leaves the hospital, or even recommending a doctor's visit; it's all counted. These regulations are not going to wring out the fraud, waste, and abuse. No, they are going to force these hospitals to provide a lower standard of care: Nurses spread thinner, less cleaning of rooms, waits for MRIs, less physical therapy, and most significantly, higher death rates.

McCaughey also said that Section 4105(a) of the Obamacare law

... provides that the secretary of Health and Human Services, in collaboration with the U.S. Preventive Services Task Force, can modify or eliminate preventive services for seniors based on that task force's recommendation. This is the task force that won notoriety last year for recommending that women 74 and older no longer get annual routine mammograms. So, in fact, seniors are in danger of losing their access to routine colonoscopies or mammograms.

Most of the seniors who will die early deaths due to the Obamacare law will be God-fearing Christians and others who had a traditional Christian upbringing and education, those who revere the Bible and our Constitution, and who remember when the United States was a freer and greater country. In my opinion, this is deliberate.

The evidence is clear: The Obamacare law is one of the most wicked and evil pieces of legislation every passed by Congress and upheld by the Supreme Court in the history of our nation.

➤ **$1 Trillion Obamacare Tax Hike Hitting on Jan. 1**
(Americans for Tax Reform, December 28, 2012)—Oblivious to many Americans, the Obamacare law contains millions of dollars of new taxes which will be most hurtful to those

making below $200,000 a year. Although Americans of all backgrounds will suffer under these taxes, they are particularly upsetting to Christians who are increasingly being taxed to support policies and programs directly opposed to Judeo-Christian principles and beliefs.

> **Free Sterilizations Must Be Offered to All College Women, Says HHS**
(CNSNews.com March 17, 2012)—Health and Human Services secretary Kathleen Sebelius announced in March 2012 that all health insurance plans for students must include free sterilizations for young women. Why would any United States government official want to encourage young women to sterilize themselves so they could never have children? This is completely against God's plan for mankind and the family.

> **Obamacare's IPAB: When Government Takes Over Health Care, You Become a Budget Item**
(CNSNews.com, October 15, 2012)—Dr. Mark Neerhof, a physician, warned what would happen to seniors and the elderly under the Obamacare IPAB Panel. Dr. Neerhof says that this board of fifteen unelected bureaucrats will make decisions that will create rationing of care, patient care based on money instead of what is best for the patient, and the slashing of Medicare reimbursements to doctors, resulting in poor care and increase of early deaths for American seniors.

> **Funds Run Low for Health Insurance in State "High-Risk" Pools**
(*Washington Post*, February 16, 2013)—The president and Democrats promised over and over again that Obamacare would provide health insurance coverage for all Americans

with pre-existing conditions who currently could not obtain health insurance. Only 100,000 Americans have signed up for this provision of the Obamacare law, and the fund is already almost bankrupt, so the Obama administration has had to reject any more applications to this fund. Officials promised that those already signed up for the program would not be affected, but this is hard to believe if funds are already so low for the program that they have had to close it to new applicants. The Obamacare law will not fully become operational until 2014, and the program is already a huge failure.

In 1792, James Madison wrote a short, two-page treatise called "Property." Madison observes that property is more than just ownership of a house, real estate, or possessions—it also includes a person's religious beliefs, conscience, and physical body. According to Madison, these are all the properties of each person, and no government has the right or authority to trample on or seize these rights from any citizen.

Madison writes:

> In the former sense, a man's land, or merchandize, or money is called his property. In the latter sense, a man has a property in his opinions and the free communication of them.
>
> He has a property of peculiar value in his religious opinions, and in the profession and practice dictated by them. He has a property very dear to him in the safety and liberty of his person. He has an equal property in the free use of his faculties and free choice of the objects on which to employ them. In a word, as a man is said to have a right to his property, he may be equally said to have a property in his rights.

Where an excess of power prevails, property of no sort is duly respected. No man is safe in his opinions, his person, his faculties, or his possessions. ... Government is instituted to protect property of every sort; as well that which lies in the various rights of individuals, as that which the term particularly expresses. This being the end of government, that alone is a *just* government, which *impartially* secures to every man, whatever is his *own*.

Madison goes on to chastise a government that refuses to protect a citizen's property, whatever that property entails.

According to this standard of merit, the praise of affording a just securing to property, should be sparingly bestowed on a government which, however scrupulously guarding the possessions of individuals, does not protect them in the enjoyment and communication of their opinions, in which they have an equal, and in the estimation of some, a more valuable property.

More sparingly should this praise be allowed to a government, where a man's religious rights are violated by penalties, or fettered by tests, or taxed by a hierarchy. Conscience is the most sacred of all property; other property depending in part on positive law, the exercise of that, being a natural and unalienable right. To guard a man's house as his castle, to pay public and enforce private debts with the most exact faith, can give no title to invade a man's conscience which is more sacred than his castle, or to withhold from it that debt of protection, for which the public faith is pledged, by the very nature and original conditions of the social pact. ...

If there be a government then which prides itself in maintaining the inviolability of property; which provides that none shall be taken *directly* even for public use without indemnification to the owner, and yet *directly* violates the property which individuals have in their opinions, their religion, their persons, and their faculties; nay more, which *indirectly* violates their property, in their actual possessions, in the labor that acquires their daily subsistence, and in the hallowed remnant of time which ought to relieve their fatigues and soothe their cares, the influence [inference?] will have been anticipated, that such a government is not a pattern for the United States.

Although I am sure Madison never imagined that the United States would ever have a government this extreme, he describes exactly what is currently happening in our country under Obamacare—and condemns it as evil.

Chapter 13

Christian Cleansing in the News Media

A book on Christian cleansing in America would not be complete without some reference to the most effective agent in Christian cleansing: the news media. I can well remember the output and influence of the limited news sources in the 1930s. There was, of course, the *Hugo Daily News,* a four-page locally produced newspaper reporting mostly local events with a one-column editorial blaming the Depression on the Republicans, and no one who had a radio would miss the humorous news analysis by Will Rogers. Also available at the time were the latest editions of *Reader's Digest* and a few other national magazines. However, since the early 1930s the news media has become much more organized, sophisticated, and comprehensive.

The most morally and politically oriented news sources have greatly increased the control of the public mind-set. To the newspapers, magazines, radio, and other news sources has been added the greatest news control source the world has ever seen—*television.* The adage that one picture is worth a thousand words is true, and the subsequent conclusion that a moving picture is worth ten thousand words is also true. I can remember when I was in the second grade excitedly reporting to the teacher and the class that I saw a motion picture movie where the actors actually talked. Since 1932 the motion picture industry has produced thousands of movies. There have been a few movies like *The Exodus* which may have had some moral and historical value, but ninety percent or more have presented an anti-Christian lifestyle: drugs, pornography, homosexuality, etc. What you eat affects your body, and what you see, read, or hear affects your mind. Now, these thousands of movies are being shown daily over television.

There is some TV time purchased on Sunday for several good Christian presentations, and TBN produces some Christian programming, some good and some not so good. But time on TV for Christian programming has to be purchased and is very expensive, while the anti-Christian world of entertainment and psychology gets paid for its time. The average person today will watch television two hours a day, yet will not get up to attend a church service for one hour on Sunday. According to a recent poll, only eight out of one hundred prominent TV personalities that report the news and other TV programming own a Bible or have ever been to church.

General television presentations do not present the advantages of a Christian family, Christian hospitals, and other ways Christians are helping the poor and needy, or that very few young people from a Christian home steal, kill, or rob others. While Fox News does present balanced programming in most cases, most TV channels do not. Due to the amoral, non-Christian sponsorship and production of TV programming, it favors non-Christian programming.

One example is the following OneNewsNow.com item dated February 13, 2013: **"Speaker Cut from Catholic Conference by Muslim Demand."** The speaker cut was terrorism expert Robert Spencer, whom we have had on our program, yet because the Muslims didn't like him, he was cut from a Catholic conference.

How do liberal and left-wing non-Christian producers change the news to fit their own purposes? A six-page article in the September 24, 2012, edition of *Front Page Magazine* explains how and why. As explained in the article, the producers simply do not present hard-hitting speeches by conservatives, but do present the liberal views of left-wing speakers. One news media outlet omitted the report of their own female reporters being raped by Muslims.

According to a September 21, 2012, Gallup poll report, sixty percent of Americans have finally reached the conclusion that the news media is biased and controlled by left-wing sources.

One of the most savage and ruthless killers of Christians was Muhammed. Yet for fear of offending Muslims, little or nothing is presented about his beheading of thousands, including Christians, in one day. Yet NBC on February 19, 2013, presented a program, sponsored by Kmart, Sears, and J. C. Penney, concerning Jesus. The following is just part of a review of the program by AFA Action Alert:

> This past weekend, NBC's "Saturday Night Live" aired an extremely violent and gory segment mocking Jesus Christ … just for laughs. And, it's available now online thanks to Kmart, Sears, and J. C. Penney. …The trailer features Jesus and the Apostles gunning down scores of Romans. At one point, the

Jesus character slices a man's head in half. "Critics are calling it a less violent 'Passion of the Christ,'" the announcer said. "I never knew how much Jesus used the N-word."

Another report on the same show titled "NBC Declares War on Christians" by Todd Starnes states in part:

> Does NBC hate Christians?
>
> I pondered that question over the weekend as I sat on my couch and watched "Saturday Night Live" blaspheme Jesus Christ in a violent and bloody Quentin Tarantino parody—just three days after Ash Wednesday.
>
> The fake movie trailer for "Djesus Uncrossed" featured the Savior brandishing guns and blowing away Romans in classic Tarantino-style. Blood and gore and profanity spewed from flat screens from coast to coast—at one point Jesus sliced a man's head in half.
>
> … Southern Baptist spokesman [Sing] Oldham said it should come as no surprise that networks like NBC set their signs on Christians for ridicule,
>
> "Jesus said, 'the world will hate you because of my name,'" he said. …
>
> And best as I can tell, the folks over at NBC are either ideological bullies or religious bigots. Either one is enough for me to change the channel.

We reference one more piece of documentation:

> The majority of Americans still do not have confidence in the mass media to report the news fully, accurately, and fairly. The

44% of Americans who have a great deal or fair amount of trust and the 55% who have little or no faith among the most negative views Gallup has measured.

The majority of Americans (60%) also continue to perceive bias, with 47% saying the media are too liberal and 13% saying they are too conservative, on par with what Gallup found last year. The percentage of Americans who say the media are "just about right" edged up to 36% this year but remains in the range Gallup has found historically.

… Americans remain largely distrusting of the news media, with 55% saying they have little or no trust in the media to report the news fully, accurately, and fairly, and 60% perceiving bias one way or the other. These views are largely steady compared with last year, even as the media landscape continues to change rapidly.

In a report released Thursday, the Pew Research Center for the People and the Press found record-high negativity toward the media on 9 of 12 core measures it tracks. These measures may help explain some of the underlying negativity. …

We do not say that every magazine article or every TV production is biased or anti-Christian, yet the overall picture in the general supervision of the media is in the control of those who are pursuing a Christian cleansing program to eliminate the church and Christian witness in America. Why is church attendance declining? Why are offerings to Christian causes and programming declining?

Some of the cause or blame must be appropriated to the news media under the control of those who would abolish in this nation all houses of Christian worship or references to the saving grace of God through Jesus Christ.

The associations between the major television channels—CBS, NBC, and ABC—is common knowledge. We might as well include Fox, because Fox hired Karl Rove for his political analysis of national and international news. ABC hired President Clinton's right-hand man, George Stephanopoulos, for news programs, and in February 2013 NBC hired David Axelrod, the ramrod behind the Obama political organization.

The role that Mr. Axelrod played in the Obama organization can be illustrated in the case of Larry Sinclair, a self-acknowledged homosexual and drug addict. WorldNetDaily.com reported the incident under the heading: **"Libel Case Against Obama's Gay Accuser Tossed."** It seems that Mr. Sinclair wrote in his book about Obama that he took drugs with Mr. Obama and had homosexual relations with him. Axelrod, according to WorldNetDaily, paid Sinclair $20,000 to take a lie detector test, but what Sinclair did not know was that Axelrod (evidently acting on behalf of Barack Obama) paid the man administering the test $750,000 to rig the results. Mr. Axelrod's connections to liberal and even communist publications and organizations has been well publicized.

But this is just one example (NBC hiring Axelrod) of the connections between the major news sources and the political machines that turn the economic, political, and even moral wheels of the United States. No one can be elected president without the endorsement of the news media. How else could a man who seemingly had no beginning, no birth certificate, and no Social Security number, suddenly become president and the most important, powerful individual in the world. We are not implying who or what this person may be or become, but it is evident that when people around the world see his image on television, they admire him.

In all this, the news media now controls the future of this nation. The news media have more connections with—and influence over—the majority of church members than does the pastor. News sources reported that the evangelical churches and memberships have lost a voice in the election of the president and congressional offices. This is the main reason for Christian cleansing in America.

Conclusion

In this book we have attempted to present the many different ways Christian cleansing is occurring throughout our nation—in the schools, in government, in our courts, and even in our churches. The devil's disciples are in control. A Muslim complaint gets a prominent speaker expelled from a Catholic conference. To avoid controversy, Tim Tebow cancels a speaking engagement at the First Baptist Church of Dallas because the pastor in a recent sermon on the family made some critical observations about the homosexual lifestyle.

In these days of economic uncertainty, most Christians—like everyone—are concerned about keeping roofs over their heads and a few biscuits on the table. In the churches, the Gospel of Jesus Christ has been traded for an anti-gospel, the "just get along" gospel.

Satan has his disciples in this nation who hate our Christian foundations, our churches, every Bible in every home, and every cross on every church. They hold nothing but contempt for Christians who love the Lord and obey the truth. They despise any laws or traditions based on the Word of God.

Credit is given to Thomas Jefferson for the warning: "Eternal vigilance is the price of liberty." Christians, including pastors, across this nation have gone to sleep and the devil's crowd is taking over. We have compromised the Gospel for a "just get along" testimony. Few, including pastors, are willing to contend for the faith once delivered to the saints, and our nation is sinking into the mire of this apostasy.

This is why Christian cleansing is sweeping across the nation with a wide broom. We pray that in some small way this book may help awaken some in time to save our nation.

Where the Spirit of the Lord is, there is liberty. Keep the Spirit of the Lord in your life, home, and church.

About the Authors

Noah Hutchings

Carol Rushton

Those who keep count say I have written over one hundred books, more or less. However, I think this book is perhaps the most relevant one for the times in which we live.

My daughter, Carol Rushton, who is our webmaster here at Southwest Radio Church Ministries, wrote three of the chapters (on the judiciary, abortion, and Obamacare). Carol also helped me with a great deal of the research. Carol also writes for our publications and appears on our daily program on special subjects.

I would encourage the reader to share this book with his or her pastor, congressman, or anyone in public education. The Christian cleansing process in our nation will push our beloved country into the dust of history, where others have made this same mistake.

If the reader likes—or doesn't like—this book, please give me your opinion. You may address your comments to me at P.O. Box 100, Bethany, OK 73008.

—Noah W. Hutchings

Extra copies may be ordered from

Southwest Radio Church Ministries
P.O. Box 100
Bethany, OK 73008
1-800-652-1144

2–10 copies at 20% discount off retail price
11–25 copies at 25% discount off retail price
26–50 copies at 40% discount off retail price
All orders over 50 copies at 50% discount off retail price